JONATHAN HOLT

SOMERSET
FOLLIES

This is Jonathan Holt's second book on architectural follies, the first being on Dorset whose landscape, like that of Somerset, does not need improving by the construction of follies. He also lectures on the subject, organises tours and conferences, and writes for several publications, including Follies, the organ of the Folly Fellowship, a charity dedicated to architectural conservation and appreciation. Since 1997 he has lived in Bath, the most densely follied city in Britain.

JONATHAN HOLT

SOMERSET
FOLLIES

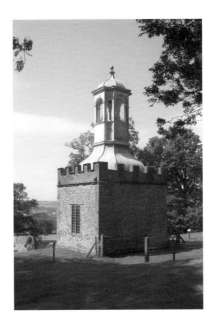

AKEMAN PRESS

Published by Akeman Press, 58 Minster Way, Bath BA2 6RL
www.akemanpress.com

ISBN13: 9780954613877

Front cover: Jack the Treacle Eater in Barwick Park

Back cover: The Boathouse Temple at Orchardleigh

Title Page: The Monmouth Tower, Chaffcombe

Printed by Short Run Press, Exeter

To
Graham Tingay (1926-2003)
who translated the Latin and Greek inscriptions
carved on the follies described in this book

Memoriae sacrum
Optimi viri...
Qui virtutem veram simplicemque colis

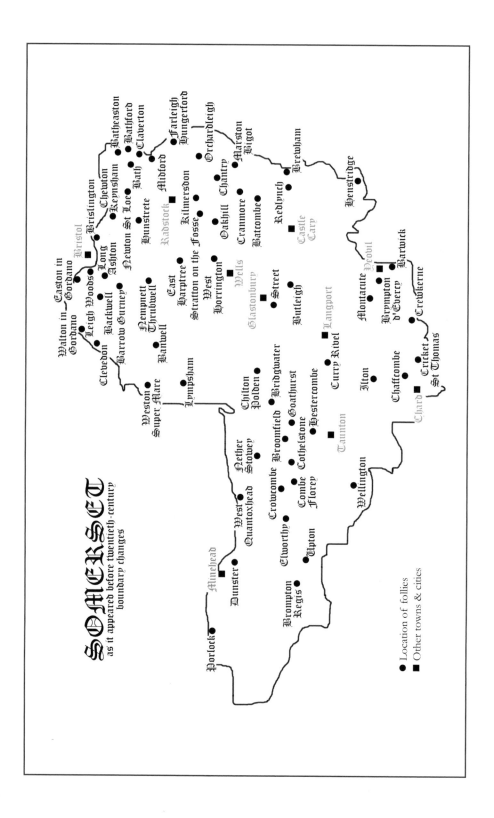

SOMERSET
as it appeared before twentieth-century boundary changes

Porlock

Minehead

Dunster

Brompton Regis

West Quantoxhead

Elworthy

Upton

Nether Stowey

Crowcombe

Combe Florey

Cothelstone

Broomfield

Goathurst

Westercombe

Wellington

Taunton

Weston Super Mare

Lympsham

Clevedon

Walton in Gordano

Easton in Gordano

Leigh Woods

Barrow Gurney

Barkwell

Barwell

Thrubwell

Pennett

Bristol

Brislington

Chewton

Keynsham

Long Ashton

Bathwell

Newton St Loe

Bathampton

Bathford

Claverton

Bath

Dunstrete

Radstock

Midford

Farleigh Hungerford

Orchardleigh

Marston Bigot

Brewham

Kilmersdon

Chantry

Oakhill

Cranmore

Watcombe

Redlynch

Castle Cary

Penstridge

East Harptree

Stratton on the Fosse

West Horrington

Wells

Glastonbury

Street

Butleigh

Langport

Curry Rivel

Alton

Montacute

Yeovil

Brympton d'Evercy

Barwick

Crewkerne

Cricket St Thomas

Chaffcombe

Chard

Chilton Polden

Bridgwater

● Location of follies

■ Other towns & cities

CONTENTS

Acknowledgements

I would like to thank the following people for their assistance in my research for this book: James Bond, David Bromwich and the Staff of the Somerset Studies Library, Roger Burton, Margaret Burrows, Mike Chapman, Dr Mary Ede, Sheila Ely, David Lambert, Stan Larcombe, Brian Lavery, Michael McGarvie, Tom Mayberry and the Staff of the Somerset Record Office, Audrey Mead, Brian Murless, Nick Owen, John Phibbs, Roger Rousell, Julian Rutter, Yvonne Sargent, Brenda Snaddon, Peter Wood and Mike Williams

Note

The inclusion of a folly or other feature in this book does not necessarily mean that there is public access to it. Many are privately owned and not usually open to visitors. While efforts were taken to ensure that any information regarding access, etc, was correct at time of publication, anyone intending to visit any of the places mentioned is advised to check details before setting out.

Introduction

It is hard to explain in a few words why Somerset has so many follies, of such varied types, spread over the greater part of the county. In fact, it is easier to start the other way round and explain how a few parts of the county have so few examples, or speculate why some styles are less prevalent than others. Exmoor, for example, has a shortage of follies perhaps because the landscape is so beautiful that it does not need embellishing and there were few major estates with money to burn on frivolities. However, moors in other regions including the neighbouring Dartmoor have considerably more follies. Chinoiserie as a style did not gain much of a foothold as it did in Staffordshire, but there was one small pagoda at Widcombe in Bath which disappeared a long time ago. Otherwise, the country is brimful with every imaginable type of folly, from towers to grottoes, from temples to columns in all sorts of styles.

The first follies to be built were the pavilions at Montacute which arrived around 1638, and then little was built until the 1740s when Charles Kemeys-Tynte started on his still numerous follies at Halswell. His friends included Henry Hoare of Stourhead and, on the other side of the Quantocks, Coplestone Bampfylde of Hestercombe. Between these and other landowners there was an exchange of ideas and inevitable copying. Soon it was as if anyone with a piece of land had to build to keep up with the aristocrats, and as one travelled across the county one was hardly out of sight of one folly before another appeared.

By the end of the eighteenth century, perhaps a hundred examples had been built in the great craze of decorating country estates. In towns, too, many appeared for a variety of reasons, or lack of reasons. Bath figured prominently as a place of decoration, not only in its architecture but also in the way its visitors showed themselves off in the facilities for entertainment and amusement. In the nineteenth century, building continued in more fitful spates, often in the form of shell houses and grottoes as at Jordans, St Audries and Pondsmead, for the Victorians of Somerset enjoyed their outhouses as much as their contemporaries elsewhere. In the twentieth century very few follies were built, and it is only really towards the close of the century that one sees a revival. The works of Graham Caine stand out as examples of original art, not only in the garden but also inside the house. While not in the classic folly mould, amateurs are also prepared to have a go at creating buildings which fit into small spaces, and Stan Larcombe, a retired man from Backwell, has shown what one can do with a glorified neo-Romanesque pot planter in the garden of his semi-detached house.

Thus folly-building continues as there will always be individuals with ingenuity who want to do something different, as well as conformists who want to copy the old styles to show off their wealth and tell everyone that they have 'arrived'. The search for these architectural frivolities can be a fascinating hobby and I hope this book will aid that search as well as be a valuable record of some fascinating, sometimes endangered, buildings.

THE FOLLIES

BACKWELL

Stan Larcombe lives in a quiet neighbourhood in Backwell and has for many years enjoyed art appreciation, attending courses and going on holiday to places such as Tuscany. Although he has no formal artistic training, in 1993 he designed a **Folly** (ST484685) that is both decorative and functional, pulling off a clever architectural coup while not upsetting the local planning authority – or his neighbours. The trick was to restrict its height to under two metres so that it is virtually invisible behind his privet hedge. Even the neighbours in the other half of his semi-detached house can only glimpse it from their upstairs windows.

Built with his own hands as a glorified flower planter, with beds in the lower parts and pots in the upper ones, Larcombe describes his folly as 'among the first in a line of Romanesque ruins'. It has a number of arches, some broken off, and liberal sculpting of breezeblocks, the main material. There are odd bits of paving stone, some decorative mouldings, and, on one wall, a face representing Gemini, the sign of the Zodiac under which both Stan and his wife June were born. It is painted pale pink and was covered with live yogurt to encourage the growth of moss. It is L-shaped, measures about six metres along one side and five along the other, and is a fine example of how anyone with a modest plot of land can build a folly which will not upset anyone and yet be a free expression of their tastes and personality.

BANWELL

An appreciation of the distant past and a love of archaeology inspired the follies on Banwell Hill, the wooded promontory at the western end of the Mendip Hills. Local farmer William Beard explored a stalactite cave here in the 1820s, which was later opened to the public by two clerical antiquarians, the local vicar, Dr Francis Randolph, and George Law, Bishop of Bath and Wells, who was also lord of the manor.

Prior to the opening, another cave was found in 1824, containing large numbers of bones from animals which had long been extinct in the British Isles, including hyena, reindeer, bison and woolly rhinoceros. A year earlier, William Buckland had published his Reliquae Diluvianae, which catalogued the animals that roamed the earth before the Great Flood. The interest aroused by this work ensured a steady flow of antiquarians and scholars to the **Bone Caves** (ST383587) at Banwell.

The first full season of visitors was in 1825. Beard was the official guide, and he took his cut of the proceeds in the form of bones for his collection. What could early visitors expect at one of the prime attractions for day-trippers from Weston-Super-Mare, five miles away? The approach from the western end of the village led the visitor through an arch, built in 1839, but accidentally demolished a few years ago by a farm vehicle. To provide food and lodging for visitors to the caves, Bishop Law built a small cottage orné, known as The Bishop's Cottage, near the entrance in 1827. This had quaint windows and a steeply-pitched

The gateway to the caves around 1910

thatched roof which nearly reached the ground and was supported by a wooden-pillared arcade. The house that Bishop Law lived in, a little further up the hill, was later extended by his son, Chancellor Henry Law. Today, it has been divided into two dwellings. Elsewhere Bishop Law created an enchanted garden with a series of buildings and sculptures, some functional, others of pure fancy.

One of them, the **Pebble Summerhouse** or Rustic Seat, is just above 'The Caves', as the main house has come to be called, and enjoys a superb view to the islands of Flat Holm and Steep Holm. Described by Beard, who built it, as 'his Lordship's curious seat above the caverns', it is a relatively straightforward structure, with three open gothic arches at the front and one at either side. It is encrusted with small round pebbles gathered from the beach at Weston-Super-Mare. The seat has gone, as has the roof, the figures of a lion and a camel that once adorned the pillars and some rustic stone pyramids. It is possible that the building was a decorated grotto, for there is reference to a 'pebble grotto' in the writings of local historian George Bennett. Barbara Jones, in Follies and Grottoes, also recorded a building whose ceiling was covered in stone chips. As it has not been possible to locate 'the pebble grotto' anywhere else, it may well have been the Pebble Summerhouse. Wherever it was, a Mr Webb ornamented its ceiling and Samuel Rodway was paid for fixing pebbles on the floor of the 'grotto' in 1833.

Two Victorian drawings, one by William Pocock of Bristol and one by an unknown artist, suggest that, if the summerhouse had a ceiling, it fell in quite early on. Neither drawing brings out the knobbly surface of the building, but both show it with pediments on four sides as well as pinnacles in the form of crosses on the apexes of the pediments and at each corner. Pocock's drawing is more detailed, showing roundels in the pediments, as well as the full extent of the house with its rustic arcade meandering along the north side, and a path running under a free-standing stone arch.

There is even greater doubt about the appearance of a building a few hundred metres to the east on Banwell Hill. This was the **Gazebo**, another summerhouse-type building, which Bishop Law moved from Banwell Camp, an ancient earthwork about half a mile east of Banwell village, in 1834. In a drawing by an unknown artist, it has a pyramidal roof with a long pinnacle at the apex. Pocock, on the other hand, shows it with an ogee-shaped roof, which gives it a Chinese look. Neither artist, however, portrays the pebbles which were used in the floor of the Gazebo. There were also iron-ore spars and stones ornamenting the ceiling, and gothic windows, some of which have survived, but without their shutters.

The Druid's Temple: harking back to gorier times

Back down the hill near the Bone Cave is the **Druid's Temple**, or Lower Grotto, which was dug out of the hillside in 1834-5. The druid vogue which had begun in the eighteenth century was still popular and, while it might seem strange for a prominent Christian to celebrate pagan culture, men of the cloth often took a scholarly interest in comparative religions. The inscription on a marble tablet outside the grotto leaves us in no doubt what Bishop Law thought about the druids, however:

Here where once druids trod in times of yore
And stain'd their altars with a victim's gore
Here now the Christian ransomed from above
Adores a God of mercy and of love

The inscription is set between two arches through which one enters a kind of snug with niches and an oval stone table, around which the druids were evidently supposed to parley and ruminate. On top is a rubble pyramid, completing a curious structure which nestles in the hillside close to the entrance to the gardens, a few paces from the entrance to the bone caves. In 1832, the bishop built a Cromlech or Trilithon in front of the Druid's Temple, but this was knocked down by army lorries in the Second World War. The Cromlech was not the only structure to be destroyed accidentally. Apart from the archway at the entrance to the gardens, there was also a **Temple**, which consisted of a portico of four Tuscan columns, a pediment with three ball finials and an ornamented ceiling. Barbara Jones, who visited Banwell around 1950, included drawings of a **Bone Chalet** and carved grotesque animals in Follies and Grottoes, while Stuart Barton, in Monumental Follies, included a photograph of **Bishop Law's Belvedere** next to the farm yard. All three structures have disappeared.

There are, however, a few remnants – little more than the foundation stones – of an **Osteon** or Osteoicon, a repository for bones. This small building, slightly ovate in plan, was decorated with spars and crystals on the outside, and had an overhanging thatched roof. There were apparently two tablets with inscriptions, probably in Latin, although Barbara Jones saw an inscription in English on what she describes as 'a coffin-shaped contemplation cosy, with a gothic façade of sandstone and plaster':

Here mid diluvial relics in this cell
Let musing heavenly contemplation dwell
And hence beholding him who reigns above
Adore a God of mercy and of love

The most enduring of Bishop Law's follies is a **Tower** (ST387587), also known as the Banwell Monument, which stands 18 metres high on a mound about 500 metres east of the caves. It has been used as a message relay-point and beacon, and in the Second World War was a look-out point for the Home Guard. A pencil drawing by John Buckler, dated September 1839, shows an obelisk on the site of the tower. There were at least ten steps leading up to the obelisk, which was built of various-coloured stone. There is no other record of this monument or what it commemorated, but, if it was still standing in September 1839, the tower, which was completed by June 1840, must have been built at amazing speed. There was originally an inscription, now lost, above the door:

The Tower in 1840   *The Tower today*

Hanice Sublime Nectice
Turrem
Georgius Henricus Law, STP
Bathoniensus et Wellensis
Episcopus
Gratus Posuit
Anno Domini
MDCCCXL

The gist of this inscription, in not the best Latin, is that George Henry Law, Bishop of Bath & Wells, uplifted the tower in a gratifying way in 1840. It is said that, when the bishop was in residence at Banwell, a servant would watch from the tower for a signal from Wells, 15 miles to the south-east, informing the bishop that his presence was required.

The tower is octagonal and built of local Knightcott lias with freestone dressings. It has three relatively wide stages, each with one window, as well as a high parapet with pinnacles protecting a fourth, narrower stage. This was a belfry from which a peal was rung to celebrate the tower's completion in 1840. A short spire which terminated in a ball finial collapsed in 1976. There were also pairs of druidical standing stones leading to the Tower, but most of these have disappeared.

Henry Law finished working on the garden around 1840 and died in 1845. William Beard continued to manage the estate as a tourist attraction until about 1865. In 1978, after passing through various hands, the estate was acquired by Ronald & Yvonne Sargent and John & Margaret Haynes who took on the mammoth task of preserving the follies. Through a series of government grants and fundraising ventures including open days, progress has been made towards stabilising the decaying structures and restoring them to their former glory.

Having no connection with Bishop Law's estate, and built shortly after his death, Banwell Castle (ST402586) dominates the eastern end of the village, hard by the road to Winscombe. It is a large mock medieval castle, exuding 'the true rust of the Barons' Wars' that Horace Walpole recognised as the essence of the Gothic Revival. Completed in June 1847 for Joseph Dyer Sympson and his wife Amelia, Banwell Castle was embellished by later owners, particularly Sir Elskin Baker in the 1880s. Built mainly of grey rubble stone with freestone dressings and slate, it could have been stoutly defended, having high walls running along the roads on two sides, and several high towers from which to pour boiling oil and fire objects at marauders. On the outer gate is a crest with a white horse and a white griffin rampant with the motto 'Esto Vigilans'. There is some doubt as to the authenticity and provenance of the crest, as it does not appear in any of the recognised catalogues of heraldry such as Burke's Armory, Papworth's Ordinary or the Dictionary of British Arms. This may be just one more element in the fabrication of antiquity that is evident all around the castle.

Inside, two drives lead to a courtyard by different routes, and there are various outhouses attached to the walls including a Lodge, a Potato House and a Coach House. The Victorians loved to play medieval games, and the Castle is full of features such as turrets, crenellations, false arrowslits, large fireplaces, Tudor-style doors, fine stained glass and a pair of lions rampant with swords flanking the six steps leading to the front door. The hall has an ornate hardwood surround, a large overmantel in carved oak, and a staircase leading up to a gallery.

Joseph Sympson soon tired of his creation and went off to rebuild Banwell Abbey. Nevertheless, he left behind a remarkable building, which survives today as a tea-room and guest house.

BARROW GURNEY

Barrow Court (ST515685) is a Jacobean house which was virtually rebuilt at the end of the nineteenth century by Henry Martin Gibbs, son of William Gibbs of Tyntesfield. He was a merchant banker who set about restoring the house on Arts & Crafts principles. The result is a warm building with plenty of dark oak panelling and stained glass.

Gibbs was not satisfied with rebuilding the house. He hired Inigo Thomas (1866-1950), an architect and landscape gardener who created the garden at Athelhampton in Dorset. In 1892, Thomas provided the illustrations for The Formal Garden in England by Reginald Blomfield, which contained a diatribe against the landscape and informal schools of garden design. While not especially formal, Thomas's design for Barrow Court owed nothing to eighteenth-century precedent. He worked there from 1892 to 1896, creating a very architectural garden, designed to entice and enchant rather than dazzle the visitor, in a series of discrete gardens with a delicate balance of natural and man-made features. He also juxtaposed elaborate grand set pieces with more intimate features: at one

The bust of January and a Venetian Gazebo at Barrow Gurney

end of the garden, a statue, probably of Mercury, and elaborately carved urns set in a grand niche contrast with a simple iris pond.

The principal garden buildings are a series of gazebos and summerhouses, including two identical Venetian **Gazebos** which stand some way apart from each other along the lower edge of the garden. These are simple, open-fronted buildings with steeply-sloping pyramidal roofs supported partly by two slender columns, affording views along the lawns and towards the house. Their elegance is enhanced and their height accentuated by ball finials.

At the western end of the lower lawn is a semi-circular exedra consisting of a line of twelve allegorical busts depicting the **Daughters of the Year**, or the ages of woman, with the facial features of the women gradually ageing from January to December, and each bust complemented by seasonal flowers. The busts are set on plinths, with six on either side of wrought iron gates whose piers boast urns and lions sculpted by Alfred Drury.

BARWICK

The collection of follies in **Barwick Park**, just south of Yeovil, are among the most enigmatic in the county. Even the date of their construction is disputed. While they are generally reckoned to date from the 1770s, it has been suggested they were built in the 1820s by the Messiter family to relieve unemployment in the Yeovil glove trade. However, when Barbara Jones visited Barwick House, she saw two paintings dating from the 1780s, featuring John Newman and his wife, who owned Barwick at the time, with the follies clearly visible in the background.

It seems likely, therefore, that John Newman built the follies around 1770. Where he got the idea from or who he got to design them are both mysteries. They are classic examples of 'squire follies', built to impress the neighbours and for personal amusement. They are the purest form of folly: eccentric, with no apparent function and owing nothing to architectural precedent. It has been suggested that they were erected as boundary markers, but there is nothing to substantiate this. Another theory is that they were intended to mark the four points of the compass, centred on Barwick House. If so, Newman got his calculations wrong. Another unusual feature is that, except for a faintly-marked track from the house to the Cone and another from the road to the Obelisk, there are no traces of roads or paths leading to the follies from the house.

On the northern edge of the estate, near Two Tower Lane, is the **Fish Tower** (ST561147). As the name of the lane indicates, there was originally another tower here. It can be seen on the tithe map of 1837, about three to five metres away from the survivor. Originally both had weathervanes shaped like fish. The surviving tower has a door and slits at intervals in the façade to accommodate stairs inside, indicating that it was originally a prospect tower. The second tower seems to have disappeared by 1880; the surviving one lost its

The Fish Tower at Barwick

weathervane in stages, with the last piece of ironwork disappearing after Barbara Jones visited around 1950. What remains is a cylindrical, random-rubble tower, about 15 metres high, with a square base and a Ham stone 'capital' shaped like a well-head with decorative, tree-like mouldings.

To the west, hard by the agricultural showground, is the **Cone** (ST555143), also known as the Rose Tower or the Princess Tower. The reason for the latter names is not clear but it is plain enough to see why it is called the Cone. Like an upside-down ice-cream cone, it rises 22 metres from a three-arched drum-shaped base, past seven levels of pigeon-holes punctuating a gradually tapering random-rubble shaft which eventually reaches a ball finial. Above the arches are traces of what may have been a wooden roof. Unlike a Roman columbarium which had decent niches for doves to roost, the Cone is hollow, the holes providing little more than a temporary perch. The three pointed arches give it a slightly unstable appearance, but, of the four main follies at Barwick, it has survived almost nearly intact. This is partly due to the strength of its design, with few overhanging pieces of masonry likely to be dislodged, and partly, perhaps, to the holes which allow the wind to pass through rather than battering against the solid structure.

The Cone around 1910

Three-quarters of a mile to the south, beside the Dorchester Road, stands an **Obelisk** (ST560130) surrounded by trees. Built of smooth rubble stone and some 15 metres high, the top of the obelisk leans at an alarming angle. Its collapse, however, may not be as imminent as some fear, because it has had this precarious appearance for some years.

Nothing in the unusual nature of the three follies described so far can prepare the visitor for the sheer architectural bedlam of **Jack the Treacle Eater** (ST563142). It starts as a jagged arch of rubble, about 3 metres high, on top of which is a circular, crenellated turret which contains a single room. On its conical roof stands a statue of Mercury, the Roman messenger of the Gods, with his caduceus, or wand, in his right hand. The total height is around nine metres, with every metre exuding eccentricity.

Legend has it that the Messiter family, who inherited the estate from the Newmans through John Newman's youngest daughter, employed a messenger boy called Jack who trained on treacle to give him energy to run to London. The truth of the matter – along with Jack's identity – are lost in the mists of Barwick Park's lake. Situated at the eastern point of the compass, Jack the Treacle Eater is the most striking and enigmatic of Barwick's follies. Silhouetted against the rising sun, it makes an impressive sight in this land of undulating fields.

Jack the Treacle Eater, with Barwick House in the distance

The final pieces of frivolity at Barwick come in the form of a **Rock Arch and Grotto** (ST559142) close to the house. The two were once connected by a path running along the edge of the pond, but this disappeared when the ground level was raised in the twentieth century. The grotto used to supply drinking water to the house from a spring which rose within it. Although the spring still trickles forth, it now flows straight into the pond. Access to the grotto is down steps and into a square chamber with two other chambers leading off. The one on the right is another square chamber containing a pool. The other is a much larger circular chamber, some four metres high and six metres in diameter. A spring issues from two of the niches in the wall and fills a deep circular pool in the centre of the chamber. Originally, there may have been a statue here, bathed in light from an opening in the domed roof, but this has long gone. Some of the stonework, with jagged pieces pointing downwards at the apexes of the entrance and the opening above the main chamber, is similar to that on the arch of Jack the Treacle Eater. In 1996, the accumulated silt was cleared out of the grotto. Since then a new pebble floor has been laid and statues placed in the six niches. This work was carried out by John Lawrence, at the same time as he converted the house into flats and built a row of cottages in the local vernacular. The view from the grotto over the pond is now a good deal more inviting than it was in the years of neglect, and the Rock Arch, hidden for so many years, can be clearly seen.

BATCOMBE

The development of the **Westcombe** estate is shrouded in mystery, as most of the estate papers were dispersed after successive sales in the twentieth century. The owner with the greatest claim to have built the **Grotto** (ST681394) is Thomas Henry Ernst (1774-1855), who worked in the Bengal Civil Service and bought the estate from George Chalmers in 1817. By 1855, according to a sketch plan of the estate, there was a boathouse and a bath house fronting onto a lake and a pool respectively, but these have since dried up.

The house was demolished in 1956, but various outbuildings survive. The entrance porch went to Street to become Clark's Folly (qv); the stables have been

converted into a house. The Grotto does not appear on the 1855 sketch, but it is the only landscape feature to survive. It stands a few hundred metres below the stables in the middle of a wood. Passing through a pointed rubble-stone arch, one enters a kind of court, verdant and dripping with water, to find a long pool of stagnant, green water. At the far end, the grotto is set into a bank. In the middle of its ferny façade, water drips from a spring, before flowing over the rubble and tufa into the pool.

The grotto can be entered from either end: from the right the open archway leads into a chamber containing a recently-added statue of a nymph, with a shallow pool in front. There may at one time have been a tunnel behind the statue, which has been blocked off. There are several rubble-lined niches before one leaves the grotto at the far end through an arch. Like many grottoes, it is hard to date due to the rubbly nature of its stone and unkempt appearance.

BATH

To build, to plant whatever you intend,
To rear the column, or the arch to bend.
To swell the terrace, or to sink the grot;
In all, let Nature never be forgot.
Consult the Genius of the Place in all.

The final line of this quotation from Alexander Pope's Epistle to Lord Burlington became one of the maxims of the landscape garden movement. After finding a site which, in the words of Lancelot Brown, had 'capability', the landscape was rearranged and trees planted to enhance its picturesque character, or, in Pope's words, to make it look 'like a landscape hung up'. The final touch was to set follies on high points or along sinuous paths. Although Pope's lines were not written specifically about Bath, he could well have had the city in mind. He was friendly with Ralph Allen whose mansion at Prior Park was built to show off the properties of Bath stone. When Allen landscaped the combe below the mansion, it was to Pope that he turned for advice.

Allen and Pope were not the only ones who saw the potential of the landscape around Bath. With its steep hills, deep combes and leafy glades, it was ripe for development by followers of the landscape movement. As London society descended on the city to take its curative waters, they brought their manners, their styles and their money.

Classical antiquity was in fashion across Europe in the eighteenth century, and as Bath was developed by architects like John Wood and his son, classical orders were adapted to an English townscape. In between the formal terraces, there was room to give vent to a little architectural frivolity, and an eclectic range of architectural styles resulted.

Some of Bath's eighteenth-century follies have long gone. At the back of Bayntun's Bookshop in Manvers Street is the site of **Marchant's Folly** (ST753644). Richard Marchant, who died in 1727, was a Quaker and Merchant Taylor. He acquired the land here, then known as Ham Gardens, and built a house with a folly nearby. A rough plan has survived, showing it to have had an irregular ground plan and a circular turret on the south side. It was probably a gazebo or summerhouse. Marchant's house was demolished in the early twentieth century, but whether the folly survived that long is not known.

Jeremiah Peirce, the first surgeon appointed to the Mineral Water Hospital, lived, as befitted a pillar of the community, in John Wood's Queen Square. In 1738, he commissioned Wood to build him a country retreat on Lansdown, where he could hold wild parties. This was **Lilliput Castle** (ST725706), a 'box' in the Doric style, which Wood's biographers, Tim Mowl and Brian Earnshaw, describe

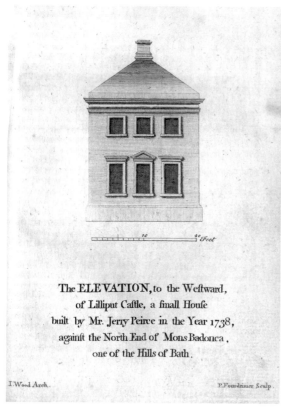

The ELEVATION, to the Weftward,
of Lilliput Caftle, a fmall Houfe
built by Mr. Jerry Peirce in the Year 1738,
againft the North End of Mons Badonca,
one of the Hills of Bath.

I.Wood Arch.   P.Fourdrinier Sculp.

as a 'slight and ridiculous' building. Its roof was pyramid shaped, and, as Wood failed to design an effective chimney, it caught fire on a couple of occasions. After Peirce gave up Lilliput Castle, it was absorbed into a large house nearby known as Battlefields, which still survives.

There was also a **Hermitage** near Lilliput Castle. In a painting from 1760 by Thomas Robins, it appears as a rustic hut with gothic windows, thatched roof and belfry. Such buildings were always rather ephemeral, being made of combustible materials, and the Hermitage has long gone.

Above, John Wood's drawing of Lilliput Castle; below, a sketch of the nearby Hermitage

From the lawn in front of Lilliput Castle an allée led to a structure which predated the castle and the hermitage, and has survived them both. The **Lansdown Monument** (ST723704), erected in 1720, commemorates the Civil War battle that took place here in 1643, at which the Royalist commander Sir Bevil Grenville was mortally wounded.

The Lansdown Monument

Many artists portrayed Bath in its Georgian heyday; few, though, have left such a comprehensive record as Thomas Robins, sometimes known as the Limner of Bath. Robins was particularly fond of the Gothic style; among the Gothic buildings he painted in Bath were the garden buildings behind the north block on the west side of Queen Square, long since demolished, the Gothic Lodge at Prior Park, Bishop Warburton's Monument to Ralph Allen, and the **Gothic Farm** (ST767690) at Charmy Down. Mr Nicholas, who owned the farm, also built a **Sham Chapel** with two gothic tracery windows. Judging by Robins' picture, the larger of its two windows was too high, at around ten metres, for the low building. The other window appears to have been a mock ruin with nothing behind it.

On the slopes of Lansdown, **St Catherine's Hermitage** (ST745661) was surrounded by one of Bath's most curious gardens. It was developed by the querulous Philip Thicknesse (1719-92), the son of a Northamptonshire clergyman, who acquired the nickname Dr Viper after picking quarrels with just about everyone in the city. After a chequered career, including spells as a soldier and a marine, he settled in Bath temporarily before buying the Lieutenant-Governorship of Landguard Fort near Felixstowe. There he acquired a taste for building follies in the garden of a cottage on the coast.

After resigning from Landguard Fort in 1766, he made Bath his permanent home, living in the Royal Crescent for a while before buying St Catherine's Hermitage in 1774. Situated in a deep combe between what is now Lansdown

Place West and Somerset Place, it was sheltered from the winds and prying eyes. From his study window he could see the River Avon, and he declared in his Memoirs that he considered the barges on the river as his own 'returning messengers whom I have sent forth to fetch me tea from Asia, sugar from America, wine from France and fruit from Portugal'.

St Catherine's Hermitage

He discovered several Roman coffins in the garden, one of which he earmarked for his own funeral. He also created a cave which he embellished and made into a **Monument to Thomas Chatterton**, the Bristol poet who died from an arsenic overdose at the age of 18 and became a posthumous hero of the Romantic movement. Little remains of the monument, and the cave has been blocked up, but a contemporary illustration shows that it was approached across a low bridge, and consisted of a recess accessible through an oval arch and faced with rubble stone. A smooth tapering tablet, inscribed with lines composed by Thicknesse in honour of Chatterton, supported a bust of the poet in bas relief, and the whole was crowned by a slender urn.

Thicknesse was so taken with this romantic spot that he buried both his daughter Ann, who died in 1785 at the age of 16, and his pet monkey in the cave. Some distance away, he built a hermit's hut which was occupied during the summer months.

Towards the end of the eighteenth century several pleasure gardens opened in Bath. Their designs were often inspired by fashionable gothic novels which cultivated in their readers a taste for the exotic and fanciful. **Grosvenor Gardens** (ST761662), behind Grosvenor Place on the London Road, was developed by John Eveleigh in the 1790s. The entrance to the gardens was through the archway of the hotel which formed the centrepiece of Grosvenor Place. Spaces were left on the façade of the hotel for a series of decorative cartouches, but the money ran out before they were all completed.

The entrance to Grosvenor Gardens

Having passed though the hotel, the visitor was greeted by a variety of entertainments, including orchestras, fireworks and bowling greens. There was an aviary, a temple with chimes, a cave, a grotto, alcoves and a labyrinth with two 'Merlin Swings', designed by the Belgian inventor JJ Merlin. On the far side of the river, with a ferry linking it to the gardens, was a building known as the **Folly** (ST763660). A farm building or cottage, dating from long before the gardens were conceived, it may have received some romantic embellishments to transform it into a picturesque eyecatcher.

Unfortunately, because Grosvenor Gardens were further out from the city than other pleasure gardens and prone to flooding, they soon failed as an enterprise, and closed around 1805. The Folly on the far bank survived the demise of the gardens and later became a pub known as the Folly, which remained open until it was bombed in a raid on Bath in 1942.

Bath's lost follies, although numerous, are outnumbered by those that have survived. The first, despite being virtually in the city centre, is little known. Just south of North Parade Bridge, on the west bank of the Avon, is a small stone niche with a bench. This is **Delia's Grotto** (ST753647), made of alternate tufa and ashlar blocks and terminating in a fine pointed keystone. It is not clear how it got its name, and, while the word grotto suggests that it may originally have been more than a niche, a drawing by Thomas Robins shows nothing more than the façade that exists today.

In 1708, Thomas Harrison built Bath's first assembly rooms on Terrace Walk. A parade, known as Harrison's Walks, led from the assembly rooms to the river and continued along the river bank. The grotto seems to have been built on the Walks somewhat later, as the dates 1737 and 1742 were carved on its back inside wall.

It was in this grotto that Richard Brinsley Sheridan (1751-1816) carried on a clandestine liaison with Elizabeth Linley, a celebrated singer, which led to their elopement. On their return to Bath after their marriage, Sheridan wrote a poem recalling their trysts in Delia's Grotto:

> Uncouth is this moss-covered grotto of stone,
> And damp is the shade of this dew-dripping tree;
> Yet I this rude grotto with rapture will own;
> And willow, thy damps are refreshing to me.
> In this is the grotto where Delia reclin'd,
> As late I in secret her confidence sought;
> And this is the tree kept her safe from the wind
> As blushing she heard the grave lesson I taught.
> Then tell me, thou grotto of moss-cover'd stone,
> And tell me, thou willow with leaves dripping dew,
> Did Delia seem vex'd when Horatio was gone?
> And did she confess her resentment to you? …

Delia's Grotto

And so on for another ten verses. Although perhaps not up to the standard of works like The Rivals or The School for Scandal, the poem made the grotto so famous that other grotto owners claimed the liason had taken place in theirs. The proprietors of Sydney Gardens, for example, managed to convince Pierce Egan, who published a series of Walks Through Bath in 1819, that their grotto was the one in the poem, and he recorded the claim in his book, overlooking the fact that Sydney Gardens were not laid out until almost 20 years after Sheridan's marriage.

By the time of his death in 1764, Ralph Allen was the most powerful figure and the biggest landowner in Bath. He arrived in the city from Cornwall in 1712 at the age of 19 to work in the postal service. He set about reforming the cross-posts and his innovations were so successful that they made him a fortune. He was a driving force behind the scheme to make the River Avon navigable between Bath and Bristol, a venture which considerably assisted him in his next major project – the quarrying and sale of Bath stone. From his quarries at Combe Down he built a tramway down to a wharf on the river, and, to demonstrate the qualities of the stone, he commissioned John Wood to build him a mansion alongside the tramway at **Prior Park** (ST762629).

According to Wood, Allen built Prior Park because of the low esteem in which Bath Stone was held. The common perception, in London at least, was that it was 'unable to bear any weight, of a coarse texture, bad colour, and almost as dear as Portland Stone', which was considered far superior. 'The reflections cast upon the free stone of the hills of Bath', Wood explained, 'brought him to a resolution to exhibit in a seat which he had determined to build for himself near his works, to much greater advantage, and in much greater variety of uses than it had ever appeared in any other structure'.

Prior Park – its name recalling ownership of the estate by the Abbey before the Reformation – was built in the Palladian style. On the south side is a row of six ionic columns with a plain frieze and entablature and a triangular pediment. The north side, overlooking the city, is more ornate, with enriched windows and a hexastyle portico with Corinthian columns forming the central third. Philip Thicknesse, from his Hermitage on Lansdown, described it, somewhat uncharitably, as 'a noble seat, which sees all Bath, and which was built, probably, for all Bath to see'. Despite having unrivalled views of and being visible from most parts of the city, the mansion was at the head of a steep wooded combe cutting into the hillside, giving it a feeling of remoteness and seclusion.

It was in this uncultivated combe that Allen planned his landscape garden, influenced not only by notions of classical landscape as portrayed by artists such as Claude Lorrain, Nicolas Poussin and Salvator Rosa, but also by philosophers who saw links between the landscape movement and political ideals, especially the doctrine of liberty.

One of Allen's chief advisers was the poet Alexander Pope, who had designed a garden on his estate at Twickenham, of which little except a grotto tunnel, built largely of Bath stone, remains. Pope made the first of many trips to Prior Park in 1737 and his contribution to the design of the garden included several follies.

Part of the landscape garden was a 'Wilderness', and it was here, next to a small cascade, that **Mrs Allen's Grotto** was built in the 1740s. 'The roof and sides of this sweet retreat', wrote a student at the Catholic seminary established at Prior Park in the nineteenth century, 'presented to the eye such a dazzling assemblage

The floor of Mrs Allen's Grotto

The Sham Bridge

The newly restored Cascade

of shells, fossils, minerals etc as perfectly astonished us … The floor was almost as beautiful as the roof, being composed of a curious kind of stone perforated and inlaid with pine-cones, fragments of bone etc, arranged in tasteful forms and the whole place exhibited such a profusion of ornament and such a combination of taste and skill as I had never before witnessed.'

Pope, not always the most generous of figures, was happy to acknowledge Elizabeth Allen's contribution to the grotto. In a letter of 1740, he rejoiced 'that Mrs Allen has begun to imitate the Great Works of Nature, rather than those Bawbles most Ladies affect'. The grotto was also the last resting place of Bounce, the Great Dane puppy given by Pope to Mrs Allen in 1739 and part of her gravestone can still be seen. After almost two and a half centuries of neglect, only one archway and the bases of the walls of the grotto are left standing, but painstaking work has revealed most of the amazingly intricate floor and a shed has now been built around the structure to prevent further deterioration.

Below the grotto was a serpentine lake, at the east end of which was built around

1740 a three-arched **Sham Bridge**, with the central arch having a pediment. From a distance it was intended to look like a real bridge, but the pond came to an end just beyond it. Of all the features inspired by Pope, this is the most complete survival. It may have been influenced by the rustic bridge at Sherborne, where Pope advised Lord Digby on landscape design, but as this has disappeared it is impossible to confirm this.

The lake fed an impressive **Cascade** with a 'Cabinet' or open space at its foot where visitors could stand to admire it. At the head of the cascade was a statue of Moses striking water from the rock, erected in 1741 at the suggestion of Bishop Warburton who married Allen's niece and was so fascinated by Moses that he write a book called The Divine Legation of Moses. The statue could also be seen as signifying the riches that Allen had found in the ground. The cascade, long dried up and overgrown, has recently been restored and now pours forth in all its eighteenth-century splendour.

Prior Park's most celebrated landscape feature – described by Horace Walpole as 'Palladio's theatric bridge' – was not built until 1755, eleven years after Pope's death. Although known as the **Palladian Bridge**, nothing like it can be found in Palladio's Four Books of Architecture. Richard Jones, Ralph Allen's clerk of works, based his design for the bridge on a bridge at Wilton, built around 1735-7 by Roger Morris for the ninth Earl of Pembroke. Jones's bridge, with its ionic columns, pulvinated frieze, Venetian balusters, pediments and stucco, is almost identical to that at Wilton, although the spacing between the centre columns is slightly wider.

The Palladian Bridge at Prior Park in the early twentieth century.
The ivy has since been removed.

The Gothic Temple in its original location below the Cascade, with the stream to the lower lakes running past. On the opposite page is a view of the Temple as it appears today in its new home in the grounds of Rainbow Hill House.

Although Jones, in his autobiography, claimed that he 'built Mr Allen's Bridge to my design', Tim Mowl suggests that it was actually designed by Thomas Pitt, the nephew of William Pitt the Elder, whom Allen wished to flatter, and who had connections with builders of other Palladian bridges, such as Lord Cobham at Stowe, George Lyttelton at Hagley and Richard Grenville at Wotton.

Pitt, Cobham, Lyttelton and Grenville were the so-called 'boy patriots' or Whigs whose ascendancy in the 1740s and 50s coincided with Allen's own. According to Tim Mowl, Allen pandered to the Whig fascination for garden buildings as status symbols to increase his influence with the powerful and flatter them by taking their advice.

To Allen's biographer, Benjamin Boyce, the Palladian Bridge is 'lighter and more exquisite in design than the great mansion presiding over the scene … Mysteriously satisfying in its proportions, the bridge was the jewel of Allen's estate.' Much of its effect is due to its setting at the foot of the combe, linking two tranquil ponds. From above, the two ponds appear as one. From below, the bridge compliments the Palladian mansion on the hill. One note of dissent was struck by the Reverend Richard Warner, however, who, while admitting that it had architectural merit, added that 'the incongruity of sticking a temple on a bridge, over which a wise man would pass as quickly as possible without stopping to make vows or pour out petitions, however sanctioned by the authority of practice, is too obvious to be reconciled to nature, truth or taste'.

'Capability' Brown also played a small part in the development of the gardens at Prior Park. He was paid £60 for making a survey and plan – a trifling sum when you consider that he received £500 for work at nearby Kelston Park. No survey or plan has been found, and it may have amounted to advice on a single feature.

Several garden features have disappeared. Near the Palladian Bridge was an octagonal rockwork **Thatched Cottage,** the outline of which can still be seen, with an Icehouse behind it. In the Wilderness below the Cascade was a **Gothic Temple**. This was built by Richard Jones around 1745, and was one of the earliest examples of Gothick architecture in the country. It had a short colonnade with three ogee arches along the front, a similar arch on either side, an ogee doorway and pointed-arch leaded windows. A low crenellation ran along the parapet, beneath which was a decorative frieze. It survived until 1921, when it was dismantled and rebuilt in the grounds of nearby **Rainbow Hill House** (ST766636), where it stands at the edge of a raised walk overlooking the garden. As part of the ongoing restoration of the gardens, trainee stonemasons from the City of Bath College are to build a replica of the Temple on its original site.

Many of the above follies featured on Thorp & Overton's Survey of the Manours of Ralph Allen, probably drawn in the 1760s. This map also showed a 'Castle in the Warren', better known as **Sham Castle** (ST766649). In 1755, William Pitt, who had, with Ralph Allen's support, been elected MP for Bath, wrote to Sanderson Miller, whom he called 'the Great Master of Gothick', asking him to 'call upon [his] imagination for a very considerable gothick object which is to stand in a very fine situation on the Hills near Bath'. Miller's imagination failed to respond, however, and it was another seven years before Richard Jones set to work on the Sham Castle we know today. After completing it, Jones noted in his diary: 'Built the Castle in the warren to my design, but would have built it larger for an object to be seen farther, but I was hindered by my master and other gentlemen.'

Sham Castle in the early twentieth century

It had no connection with Prior Park, being over half a mile away on Bathampton Down, and not visible from any part of the gardens. It is, however, visible from many parts of Bath — even more so than Prior Park — and the story has arisen that Ralph Allen built it as an eye-catcher to be seen from his town house in Lilliput Alley. However, not only had Allen given up the town house by this time; other buildings — notably the Parade Coffee House (now the Huntsman pub) — had sprung up in front of it, blocking the view. He probably built Sham Castle for the same reason as he built Prior Park – to show off the superior qualities of Bath Stone, especially to those London builders who still resisted using it. Curiously, however, it was originally painted white to make it even more eye-catching. The paint gradually wore off and by the end of the eighteenth century it had assumed the character of a romantic ruin.

From afar it looks an imposing building; closer inspection, however, reveals it to be no more substantial than a stage set. Although the square towers at either end have a satisfying solidity to them, those flanking the central arch, which look circular, are only semi-circular. The back of the castle is flat with only a small access door to what is essentially every child's dream of a toy fort. The parapets are crenellated and the towers sport false lancet windows. Vertical and cross-shaped arrow-slits are provided as well, although – at a quarter of a metre wide and a metre high – they would be unlikely to offer much protection. The central arch is surmounted by three sham lancet windows, the middle one of which bears the following inscription:

Erected in 1762
Sham Castle
Built by
Ralph Allen
Was Restored and Presented
With the Site now Enclosed
to the
City of Bath
by
Richard Rusden Ottley
and
Arthur Edward Withy
Citizens of Bath
in the year
1921

James H Colmer   Fred D Wardle
Mayor   Town Clerk

Jones recorded in his diary that Ralph Allen had plans for another eye-catcher, 'but I put him off that, which would have cost him £250'.

Allen died in 1764, two years after Sham Castle was completed, and after 30 years residence at Prior Park, His estate covered over 3,000 acres and extended from Bathampton in the east to Twerton in the west. Allen is often hailed as something akin to a secular saint and a role model of the benevolent businessman. The novelist Samuel Richardson and painters such as Thomas Gainsborough and William Hoare were among those who sang his praises, although his most celebrated admirer was Henry Fielding, who is said to have based the character of Squire Allworthy in Tom Jones on him. 'His house, his furniture, his gardens, his table, his private hospitality and his public benevolence', Fielding wrote of Allworthy, 'all denoted the mind from which they flowed, and were all intrinsically rich and noble, without tinsel or external ostentation'.

Philip Thicknesse offers an alternative view. 'He was said to bear his great prosperity with humility', he wrote of Allen, 'and to conduct all business with the utmost probity. That he affected a simplicity of manners and dress we can testify; but we can by no means allow that he was not a man deeply charged with pride, and without address enough to conceal it. His plain Quaker coloured suit of clothes, and shirt sleeves with only a chitterlin [frill] up the slit might, and did deceive the vulgar eye; but he could not bear to let Pope (who was often his visitor) call him what was true (low-born Allen) but made him substitute in its place, that which was false (humble Allen).'

After Allen's death, his niece Gertrude inherited the estate. When she demolished part of a Gothic Lodge overlooking the mansion, her husband, Bishop

Warburton, used some of the stone to build a **Monument to Ralph Allen** (ST765632) in Monument or 'Monny' Field, south-east of the mansion. This preserved many of the features of the original building, including the two-storeyed, triangular base with blind windows. Its shape may have been a reference to the Holy Trinity, which features in one of England's most celebrated follies, Sir Thomas Tresham's Triangular Lodge in Northamptonshire. The corners of the base were surmounted by pinnacles, linked by parapets pierced with quatrefoil openings. On top of the base was a two-storey round tower with 75 steps and a conical roof finished with an ornate pinnacle. On a slab above the door was the following inscription:

Memoriae sacrum optimi viri, Randulphii Allen
Qui virtutem veram simplicemque colis, venerare hoc saxum

which can be translated as:

You who value true and uncomplicated goodness, venerate this stone,
Sacred to the memory of a splendid man, Ralph Allen.

The tower was built by Richard Jones, although not as quickly as he would have liked, due to Gertrude Warburton finding more pressing work for him. 'She made me finish some pig-styes', he wrote in his autobiography, 'before she would suffer me to go and finish his monument, which was sore against my will, and because it took some time she begrudged every farthing that went for it'.

The monument was sometimes referred to as 'Bishop Warburton's Tower'. By 1848, Dr James Tunstall, in his Rambles about Bath, recorded that it was already 'crumbling through neglect, and promises, for want of slight repairs to become a ruin'. Although it survived for another century, by 1953 it was in such a parlous state that it was demolished. No trace of it remains.

Prior Park College, which has occupied Prior Park since 1924, donated the gardens to the National Trust in 1993. The park was overgrown and cattle grazed the slopes. The National Trust initiated a programme of restoration and a grant from the Heritage Lottery Fund enabled the project to be brought to fruition.

The most romantic member of the 'dreaming spire' school of tower builders was William Beckford (1760-1844), whose talents, accomplishments and exploits as traveller, writer, aesthete and collector are so numerous that lack of space prevents any detailed discussion here. For many years his all-consuming work was Fonthill Abbey in Wiltshire. With its vast galleries, great stained glass windows and soaring pinnacles, this great shrine to one man's ego was surmounted by a 84-metre tower. The spire he intended to build on top of the tower would have been 140 metres high, significantly higher than that on Salisbury Cathedral, but he was stopped by lack of funds. At first, the abbey was poorly constructed and there were several minor collapses. The standard of work improved, but in 1825 the central tower dramatically collapsed. Until recently, it was thought this was due to inadequate foundations, but it is now known that they were substantial enough to support the weight of the masonry. Instead, it had been built too tall and had simply collapsed under its own weight, bursting outwards. What remained of the abbey was finally demolished after 1858 – except for one small section, the Lancaster Tower. It still stands, lonely and romantic, brooding over the site of this greatest of follies.

In 1822, despite finding the city 'dingy and wretched', Beckford moved to Bath. He bought 20 Lansdown Crescent, as well as a tract of land a mile and half long leading to the top of Lansdown. In 1825, he engaged Henry Edmund

Goodridge, the son of a local speculative builder, who had already done work for him at Lansdown Crescent, to build him a tower on Lansdown. Like Fonthill Abbey, the construction of **Beckford's Tower** (ST737675) was not without its hitches. When the builders engaged to build it learned of Beckford's homosexual affair with a young boy, 'Kitty' Courtney, at Powderham Castle some 40 years earlier, they downed tools. Goodridge persuaded them to return to work, however, and the basic frame of the tower was completed in a matter of weeks.

Goodridge's first design was for a 'Saxon Tower'. Beckford appears to have rejected this, even though it was based on a sketch he himself had made on the edge of a newspaper. Next, Italian Romanesque decorations were added to the original design. It was not until Goodridge opted for an Italianate style, however, that Beckford gave him the go-ahead.

Approached by a flight of steps leading up to a three-arched loggia, the tower was built in three progressively narrow stages. Before remodelling, the ground floor housed a bedroom and kitchen, a pump room to provide heating for the tower and a mortuary chapel with a bay window. The second storey comprised a suite of elegantly furnished rooms which housed part of Beckford's art collection. Out of the roof of this block jutted two chimneys joined by an arch.

Rising from the main building was the tower. The original intention was that it should be square and unadorned, culminating in a deep Doric entablature with a projecting cornice, above which would be the roof. The story has long been told that Beckford, dissatisfied, cried, 'Higher!' and restoration work on the tower has shown that this is no mere legend. Goodridge added a 'Belvidere' – Beckford's preferred spelling – from which Beckford could admire the views in all directions. Above the first cornice three tall recessed windows looked out on each side. The entablature to this stage has a dentilled cornice and blocking course ornamented with panels of Greek key fret, topped by a parapet which has a square block with roundel ornamentation at each corner.

Beckford was still not satisfied. At this point Goodridge possibly suggested an idea he had designed as early as 1817. Proposed as a monument to Princess Charlotte, it had a structure based on the Choragic Monument of Lysicrates in Athens, placed on an octagonal plinth. Beckford approved and it became the crowning lantern to the tower. Its eight fluted columns, made of gilded cast iron, are encircled by an octagonal parapet with urns at each corner, and it is topped with a gilded ball finial. This unique fusion of Greek and Italian, of the Picturesque and the Sublime, was never repeated in Britain.

The lantern rises to 47 metres, 240 metres above sea level. However, it was not completed until 1827, two years too late for Beckford to look across to the tower at Fonthill, 25 miles to the south-east, which had fallen down nearly two years earlier. Nevertheless, he was able to ascend the tower and read his magnificent collection of books, reliving, albeit on a more modest scale, the despotic seclusion he had espoused in his Wiltshire wilderness.

The interior of the tower was lavishly furnished. The Scarlet Drawing Room had leaded windows, a marble chimney piece, elaborate drapery and chairs padded with velvet, as well as a selection of exquisite paintings and objets d'art. At the end of a vaulted corridor, richly panelled and sculpted with bas reliefs of cherub's heads, was a statue carved by Rossi of Beckford's patron saint, Anthony of Padua, holding the infant Jesus and backed by a slab of red porphyry with an inlaid frame of green marble surrounding it. From here, 154 spiral stairs led up to the Belvidere. This too was richly decorated with woven damask curtains and ornate plasterwork.

In the late 1990s, it became apparent that, unless urgent remedial action was taken, the lantern, and possibly the tower itself, would collapse. The Bath Preservation Trust, which owned the building, spent £680,000 on a rescue package. Not only was the lantern saved, its columns were re-gilded, the iron grille running round the top restored, and the ball finial replaced. The opportunity was also taken to restore the interior of the tower to something approaching what it looked like in Beckford's day, using a series of paintings commissioned by Beckford from Willes Maddocks shortly before his death in 1844. The lower part of the building, which was restored with the help of a grant from the Landmark Trust, is now a holiday flat.

Beckford also paid great attention to the approach to the tower from Lansdown Crescent. Full of incident and surprise thanks to his embellishments and landscaping, it became known as Beckford's Ride, and it was along this route that he rode his Arab mare on a daily basis for many years. Over 400 men were engaged to build walls and paths along the route as well as plant trees and landscape the area.

Approaching the tower from Lansdown Crescent, the first major structure was an **Embattled Gateway**, whose door Henry Goodridge designed a little too low for most riders on a full-sized horse to pass through without dismounting, despite a contemporary illustration by Willes Maddox which shows a man in a top hat riding through it. The path up to the gateway ran between low walls and on either side of the gateway were two plain low arches.

Beckford's Embattled Gateway

In the opinion of the artist Henry Venn Lansdown, the Embattled Gateway was erected 'chiefly to shut out the view of an unpicturesque object', although he did not specify what this was. It also marked the transition from the enclosed garden to open country. Beckford also indulged his interest in heraldry, adorning the gateway with the coat of arms of a family with which he had no connection. The door was studded with heavy nails and the top of the gateway was crowned by machicolations and crenellations, giving it a medieval air, heightened today by the ivy which has grown over it.

Near the top of the ride was a Dyke Garden, with an Italianate villa, which disappeared in 1851, and the entrance to a **Grotto Tunnel**. Beckford, always a very private man, wanted to avoid being seen on his way up to the tower, and he built this tunnel, with a pool of water near the entrance, to avoid crossing a public right of way.

At the far end of the tunnel a flight of rusticated steps led up to the grounds surrounding the tower. Henry Venn Lansdown, in his Recollections of the Late William Beckford, recalled meeting Beckford here: 'We turned a corner, and Mr Beckford stood before us, attended by an aged servant, whose hairs have whitened in his employment, and whose skill has laid out these grounds in this beautiful manner. Mr Beckford welcomed me in the kindest way, and immediately began pointing out the various curious plants and shrubs.' The servant was Vincent, the gardener that Beckford had brought with him from Fonthill, and the curious plants and shrubs included Irish yews, American maples and a Chinese rose tree.

Beckford died in 1844, and, despite his wish to be buried next to his tower, was interred in the Abbey Cemetery in Widcombe. However, when the grounds became a cemetery a few years later, his body was moved and now lies in the shadow of the tower, raised above the ground in a sarcophagus of pink basalt like the Saxon kings from whom he claimed ancestry. 'Eternal Power!', reads one of the plaques on his tomb, 'Grant me through obvious clouds one transient gleam of thy bright essence in my dying hour'. The other records that he was 'late of Fonthill … enjoying humbly the most precious gift of Heaven – hope'.

The last word, though, should rest with Henry Venn Lansdown, who evokes the impact of this extraordinary tower:

> The effect of the building is grand and stately beyond description. The long line of the flat distance and the flatness of the Down here come in contact with the perpendicular line of the Tower and lower buildings, producing that striking combination which never fails to produce a grand effect. This is the real secret of Claude's seaports. His stately buildings, moles and tall towers form a right angle with the straight horizon; thus the whole is magnificent. Nothing of the sort could be produced in the interior of a country but in a situation like the present. Who but a man of extraordinary genius would have thought of rearing in the desert such a structure as this, or creating such an oasis?

Because it sits in the garden of Beckford's house at 20 Lansdown Crescent, it was long believed that the **Islamic Summerhouse** (ST746661) was built by him. However, an 1886 Ordnance Survey map shows no building on the site of the summerhouse, although a later edition, published in 1903, shows it clearly. This indicates it was built by Captain Frederick Huth, a keen orientalist, who lived at 20 Lansdown Crescent in the late nineteenth and early twentieth centuries. Huth had a reputation for rescuing threatened buildings, but it is not known whether the summerhouse originally stood somewhere else. However, deficiencies in its construction, such as some of the bricks jutting out from under the coping stones, suggest that it is a rebuild. Bath historian Kirsten Elliott, who has researched the building, points out it might have come from somewhere on the Beckford

The Islamic Summerhouse

estate, although it has been suggested that it actually came from the gardens of the British Embassy in Istanbul. We may never know.

The summerhouse stands in the far corner of the garden abutting the wall of No 19. It displays many Moorish features such as a domed roof. The architrave of the door on the west side is decorated with a pink and white trefoil pattern, and has small niches on either side. A large semi-circular headed window on the south, decorated with a similar pattern, is flanked by two smaller windows.

The three-metre-high gateway known as **Pinch's Folly** (ST754656) on Bathwick Street was probably erected in the 1830s to form the entrance to John Pinch's building yard. The gateway is surmounted by an urn on a double

scroll arch, has a carved shield on its keystone and four small, animal heads jutting out of the façade. As the stone has worn away, the precise nature of these beasts is unclear. Near one of the heads is an enigmatic inscription – P36ft. It has been suggested that this means 'Pinch 1836 fecit' – or in other words 'Made by Pinch in 1836'. This would tie in with the likely date of its construction, although the style of the archway suggests a much earlier date. It is possible that it came from somewhere else – an early instance of architectural reclamation – and this would also explain why something so elaborate was erected at the entrance to a builder's yard. The yard has, however, long gone and a modern block of flats now occupies the site, with the folly standing rather incongruously in front of it.

Although the craze for building grottos had abated somewhat by the early nineteenth century, it did not totally disappear. In 1836, General Augustus Andrews, retiring to Bath after a distinguished army career, built a Greek Revival villa on Sydney Road, naming it **Vellore House** after an Indian garrison town. The architect is unknown, although it has been suggested that it was John Pinch.

General Andrews spent vast sums on landscaping the grounds, importing exotic species of shrubs and trees including gingko biloba. It is rumoured that the **Grotto** (ST759653) he built on the lawn a couple of hundred metres below the house and close to the public road cost in excess of £1,000. Around four metres high and surrounded by a circle of stones, it is built of tufa and rough-cut Bath stone, giving it a jagged appearance. There is an arch on either side and a fishpond, built of tufa, on the side facing the house. Inside are three niches surrounded by ferns, into which water trickles from a tank above. Although lit by unglazed, wrought-iron windows, with panes of glass in the centre of the roof, the overall effect is extremely gloomy, and there are rumours of ghostly lights having been seen flickering from within and a woman's voice calling out. When the house was sold after General Andrews' death, however, the grotto was described as 'a place where in the heat of summer the most delicious quietitude [sic] may be enjoyed'.

In 1990, the grotto was restored at a cost of £9,500 – very reasonable compared to the £26M spent transforming Vellore House, which had been a nurses' home for many years, into the Bath Spa Hotel. Dave Ellis, who restored it,

The grotto at Vellore House in the early twentieth century

reckoned that the design of the grotto indicated it was the work of Josiah Lane of Tisbury, who designed grottos and garden features at Bowood, Fonthill, Wardour Castle, and elsewhere. However, this would mean that it was constructed in the late eighteenth century – and this raises the intriguing possibility that it started life elsewhere.

On the other side of Sydney Road from Vellore House are Sydney Gardens (qv), whose attractions included 'Merlin's Cave', which disappeared when the Great Western Railway was built through the Gardens in 1840. Whether Merlin's Cave was by Josiah Lane, and whether it was moved to Vellore House in 1840 must remain fascinating hypotheses until something substantial in the way of evidence turns up. The only hint that the grotto may once have been in Sydney Gardens is a row of tufa blocks, similar to those used in the grotto, lining a path in the gardens. Did they come from the grotto when it was dismantled, or is their presence there merely coincidental?

Sydney Gardens (ST757653) opened in 1795 as Bath's newest visitor attraction, rivalling the long-established Spring Gardens on the east bank of the Avon near Pulteney Bridge. Designed by Thomas Baldwin, who also built Great Pulteney Street, the pleasure gardens and the Sydney Hotel were taken forward after his bankruptcy by Charles Harcourt Masters. The gardens were a place of genteel entertainment. The amusements laid on for those who could afford the price of entry included a labyrinth, a ruined castle, a hermit's cot, a water wheel, an artificial cascade, and a 'capital swing of Merlin's construction'. This was the brainchild of JJ Merlin, a Belgian inventor who played on the coincidence between his name and that of King Arthur's mentor by dressing up as a wizard and casting spells in the grotto which may have found its way into the grounds of the nearby Bath Spa Hotel.

At the top of the gardens was a semicircular loggia, which was rebuilt in 1836, probably by John Pinch the Younger, to form part of a new building called Sydney House. It was flanked by two curving wings, but these were demolished in 1938 when the loggia was substantially rebuilt, amid howls of protest, by Bath Corporation.

Above, an early twentieth-century view of the loggia at the top of Sydney Gardens; on the left, shorn of its wings, the same building today

Bath Corporation had taken over the gardens to develop them as a municipal park in 1909. One of their first shows of municipal munificence was the building of the **Temple of Sul Minerva**, which was used as an advertisement for Bath at the Festival of Empire Exhibition at Crystal Palace in 1911. When the exhibition closed, the Parks and Cemeteries Committee debated whether the £288 costs of removal were too high, but eventually agreed to bring it back to Bath. It lacks its original mosaic pavement, but it acquired a plaque commemorating the 1909 Bath Pageant, which is something of a red herring. The story goes that the Bath Pageant Committee was looking for somewhere to commemorate the pageant, which had been held in Royal Victoria Park, but could find nowhere suitable to mount the plaque. More than two years after the event, they eventually settled on the Temple of Sul Minerva, but

The Temple of Sul Minerva at the 1911 Festival of Empire

failed to include the information that the pageant took place elsewhere, with the result that many people have come to believe that the pageant was held here with the temple as the centrepiece of the event.

The Temple after relocation to Sydney Gardens

The Temple commemorates Bath's healing waters, and its name combines the Celtic and Roman gods of healing. It is a reproduction of the Temple of Sul Minerva that lies beneath Stall Street in Bath, and recent computer projections show that it is remarkably faithful to the original. In Corinthian Tetrastyle with a substantial interior behind an open portico, it has a finely executed tympanum with the Gorgon-like head of Sul or Sulis between two supporting female figures.

Bath Corporation mounted a similar publicity exercise for the British Empire Exhibition at Wembley in 1924, for which local builders constructed a model of the King's Spring and a pavilion. At the end of 1925 the **Wembley Pavilion** was brought back to Bath and re-erected at the north-east corner of the Botanic Gardens in Royal Victoria Park (ST739655). It has three curved open-fronted arches supported by double columns, a parapeted flat roof and glazed windows on either side flanked by pilasters. 'Aquae Sulis', the Roman name for Bath, is carved on the parapet along with the city's coat of arms. A plaque records that:

This building was originally erected by
the Corporation of Bath at Wembley in 1924 for
THE BRITISH EMPIRE EXHIBITION
and was re-erected on this site in 1926
when the Botanic Garden was extended

J. Basil Ogden   Cedric Chivers
Town Clerk   Mayor

The Wembley Pavilion after relocation to Bath's Botanic Gardens; inset, how it originally appeared at the British Empire Exhibition at Wembley in 1924

The exhibit cost the ratepayers just over £2,115, but was good value, as many tourists, and even new residents, came to Bath after seeing such an attractive advertisement at Wembley. However, when it was moved to Bath, surrounded by a rockery and water features, the set-up was condemned by many for its bleakness. As the plants have grown up around it the garden designer's vision has been amply vindicated. In 2007, it was announced that the Pavilion would be developed as an education centre.

Blaine's Folly (ST741665), a 35-metre tower on the slopes of Lansdown, was built by Sir Robert Stickney Blaine in the 1880s as an unemployment relief measure, with 250 men engaged on its construction. The architect is

Blaine's Folly from the west

unknown, although Blaine may have designed it himself, using Beckford's Tower at the top of the hill as a model.

Blaine came to Bath in the 1860s. By 1872 he was Mayor, in 1885 he became a Member of Parliament, albeit for only a year, and in 1896 he was knighted. He owned the Summerhill Park estate which contained a large mansion, now demolished, and grounds stretching up to the tower. When

he died in 1897, an obituarist described him as 'the most modest, unassuming and diffident of men. He would disparage his own qualities and powers, and would deprecate eulogy of himself ... How true, pure, and good that character was!'

The tower is now owned by Kingswood School. Until the 1950s it was used as a prefects' den, where no doubt the boys whiled away their hours drinking dandelion and burdock over the Beano in the two rooms at the top. Growing concerns over health and safety and deterioration of the structure, including the loss of part of the parapet, have since led to it being sealed off.

Crowe Hall (ST760639) was built in the mid-eighteenth century for Brigadier Crowe on a slope overlooking Widcombe Manor. In the nineteenth century, George Hayward Tugwell laid out the gardens, dotted with statues, urns and other ornaments. A **Grotto** below the house was probably built by William Carmichael (1816-1904), who moved from Sandringham in 1874 to become Tugwell's head gardener.

The grotto has several entrances, but perhaps the most agreeable approach is from the top. Here you have a choice of two archways, both leading to a flight of steps which descend between walls studded with ammonites. At the bottom is a roofless court with three arches leading out into the garden. Parts of the grotto incorporate bits and pieces of old buildings, including, so it is said, a section of the old East Gate of the city of Bath. A journalist writing in the Journal of Horticulture and Home Farmer in 1906, only 30 years or so after it was built, had this to say about it:

Pretty grottos intercept the way leading one from one terraced level to another, and in passing the visitor's notice is arrested by an inspection of what was once a gateway of the ancient walled city, cunningly adapted to the private entrance to this pretty grottoed pathway. The age of this relic was not ascertained, but it must date back some hundred years.

The Grotto at Crowe Hall

Below Crowe Hall lies **Widcombe Manor** (ST759638), the core of which was probably built by Scarborough Chapman around 1690. The house was inherited by Philip Bennet of Maperton, who had married Chapman's daughter Jane in 1702. His son, Philip Bennet the Younger, rebuilt the house in 1726-7. The architect is unknown; Richard Jones, Nathaniel Ireson and Thomas Greenway have all been put forward as candidates, but the most likely contender is John Strahan, who built houses in a similar style in Bristol, as well as Frampton Court near Gloucester, which has a staircase like that at Widcombe.

The provenance of the garden buildings at Widcombe is even more problematic. The first which strikes the visitor is the **Summerhouse**, a fine eighteenth century building which was moved here from a small estate at Freshford on the Wiltshire border in 1975. On either side of the semi-circular-headed front door are Doric columns where plain stone alternates with vermiculated tufa. To the side are oeil de boeuf windows, and above is a simple classical frieze and entablature. The building has a domed skylight, probably a recent addition, and two rubble-stone chambers.

The Summerhouse at Widcombe Manor

The Grotto and Cascade at Widcombe Manor

The path beside the Summerhouse leads down to a **Grotto**. This has an arched entrance, about two metres high, built of rubble and tufa stone, with an iron gate. Steps lead down to a spring flowing from the back wall, close to which is a small opening. The water then falls into a small basin and on into a curious arrangement of water channels in the limestone floor. There is also an unfilled niche on the left, the purpose of which is unclear. The psychological impact of the grotto is muted, and it does not inspire melancholy or contemplation. In 1999, its structure was stabilised and the water flow was restored to the nineteenth-century pools some 40 metres down the slope.

From here one soon reaches a circular lake which covers around 100 square metres. On the south side is a **Cascade** made of massive boulders, with square niches on either side. The top of the cascade has a viewing platform with seats on either side, where, if you look carefully, you can still make out one of the feet of a statue of Neptune set on a dolphin's head. The statue can be seen in a rather hazy nineteenth-century engraving.

South of the cascade is a **Mount**, around six metres high, with a spiral path leading to the summit, on which, according to a drawing from the 1750s by Thomas Robins, once stood a Chinese pavilion. However, there is evidence to show that the drawing may be of the grounds of Lyncombe Spa, a nearby pleasure garden which also sports a mound.

The kitchen garden of Widcombe Manor used to lie on the other side of Church Street, in what is now the garden of **Widcombe House**. The most glorious of the outbuildings here is a twelve-metre-high octagonal **Dovecote** which Peter

An early twentieth-century view of the Dovecote from the grounds of Widcombe Manor

and Jean Hansell describe as 'the quintessence of all other in terms of elegance and ingenuity of design'. It is unique in having three storeys and uncommon in having both exterior and interior pigeonholes, as well as living accommodation for humans. The two lower floors, both of which have fireplaces, are connected by a spiral stone staircase. Access to the upper floor is either through the ceiling of the floor below or up an external ladder. The roof is surmounted by a domed belfry topped by a ball finial and weathercock. The architect is unknown, but John Strahan must once again be a strong contender.

Abutting the east wall of the garden is a **Grotto** built mainly of tufa and probably dating from the mid-eighteenth century. Rising to about four metres, it is unusually high for a grotto. A rough-arched entrance leads into a square barrel-vaulted chamber with a semi-circular-headed niche in the back wall, into which a mirror and a wood carving of an exotic god was inserted in the late twentieth century. There are also traces of a blocked-up doorway in the south-east wall and a niche in the north-west wall.

The Dovecote and the Garden House at Widcombe in the early twentieth century

At the northern end of the property, abutting a wall and close to the street is the **Garden House**. It is a simple two-storey building with three semi-circular-headed doorways with keystones in their arches, separated by columns, and originally had an open loggia. Mowbray Green, who made a detailed study of it around 1900, suggested that it bore a passing resemblance to the Palladian bridge at Prior Park but felt that stylistically it had an earlier date.

Bath's three obelisks all commemorate royal visits. The first, in the **Orange Grove** (ST752648), was commissioned by Beau Nash from John Wood, who estimated it would cost £8 2s. 7½d for a nine-metre column. It could have cost much more, for Nash originally wanted a 24-metre obelisk. According to JF Meehan in Famous Houses of Bath & District, it was based on a design by William Borlase, a Cornish historian who visited Bath for a cure under the direction of his relative, Dr William Oliver, in 1730. It commemorates the visit of William, Prince of Orange, to the city in 1734 and was at one time known by local wags as 'the chimney without a tun', a tun being a funnel.

The coat of arms on the Orange Grove obelisk

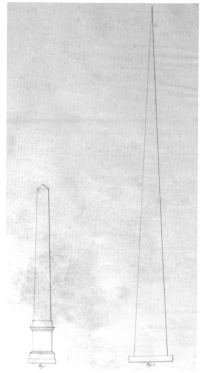

John Wood's drawings of the obelisks in
the Orange Grove and Queen Square

The obelisk in Queen Square today

The second column, also designed by John Wood, was erected in 1738 in **Queen Square** (ST748650), again at the instigation of Beau Nash, to commemorate the visit of Frederick, Prince of Wales. It bears a distinctly uninspiring inscription by Alexander Pope:

In Memory
Of Honours Conferr'd
And In Gratitude
For Benefits Bestow'd
In This City
By His Royal Highness
Frederick
Prince Of Wales
And His
Royal Consort
In The Year MDCCXXXVIII
This Obelisk Is Erected
By Richard Nash, Esq.

It was originally intended that the arms of the Prince of Wales should appear at the front and back of the obelisk, with shields on the sides and pairs of lions and unicorns round the base, but these plans were dropped for financial reasons. Wood lamented this decision, which 'deprived the City of Curious Examples for such Kind of Ornament, and robbed the Monument of its greatest Beauty'. Even without these embellishments, the obelisk cost £80 15s. 7d, ten times more than the obelisk in the Orange Grove, although, as Beau Nash pointed out, this figure was low compared to what it had cost the pharaohs to erect their obelisks in Egypt. It originally stood 21 metres high but being after being damaged in a gale in 1815 was reduced to its present height of around 18 metres.

The third obelisk, in **Royal Victoria Park** (ST743653), commemorates Queen Victoria's coming of age in 1837, the same year as her accession to the throne. As Princess Victoria, she had opened the park, the first of many to bear her name, in 1830.

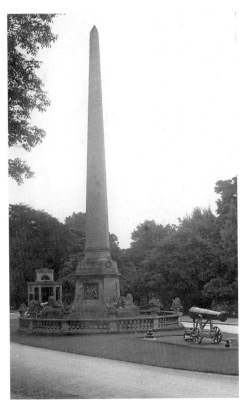

The obelisk in Royal Victoria Park in the early twentieth century

The foundation stone of the obelisk, designed by GP Manners, was laid on 24 May 1837, the day of Victoria's eighteenth birthday. It was unveiled just over a year later, on the day of her coronation, 28 June 1838.

Around 18 metres high, it is triangular and sits on a tri-axial base guarded by lions and surrounded by a circular balustrade. On each of the obelisk's three sides is a plaque with an inscription accompanied by either a royal coat of arms or a bas relief, added at later dates and recording events in the queen's life. A strip of carving runs round the bottom of the shaft and laurel wreaths embellish its corners.

After the Crimean War, the Government presented the City of Bath with two cannons captured at Sebastopol. These were inaugurated with much pomp and ceremony close to the base of the obelisk in September 1857 on the second anniversary of the Fall of Sebastopol. Unfortunately, they were removed in 1941 to be melted down for the purposes of another war, although this time the Russians were on the same side as the British.

BATHEASTON

Batheaston Villa, built in the early eighteenth century, is notable chiefly for a large bow window topped by crenellations. About 100 metres from the house, on a small mound, is **Lady Miller's Rotunda** (ST772671), a small octostyle building with Doric capitals on a plinth. Although little known today, in its heyday it was one of the most celebrated buildings in the Bath area.

After Batheaston Villa was acquired by Sir John Miller in the mid-eighteenth century, his wife, Lady Miller, proceeded to turn it into a mecca for Bath society. Such was the popularity of her Thursday gatherings that on one occasion more than 50 carriages made the trip out to Batheaston. Although Horace Walpole described the Villa as 'a very diminutive principality with large pretensions', Lady Miller's guests included such luminaries as the Duchesses of Beaufort, Cumberland, Northumberland and Ancaster.

The highlight of the gatherings was a poetry competition, in which guests with literary pretensions were invited to compose bouts rimés, or short poems ending in rhymes supplied by Lady Miller. These were written on scraps of paper and placed into a vase the Millers had picked up in Italy, which stood in a rotunda. They were then taken out and read to the assembled company, who were seated on a nearby viewing platform, which can still be seen.

Horace Walpole, writing in 1773, provided a suitably acerbic view of the proceedings:

> Near Bath is erected a new Parnassus, composed of three laurels, a myrtle tree, a weeping willow, and a view of the Avon, which has now been christened Helicon … A Roman vase, dressed with pink ribands and myrtles, receives the poetry, which is drawn out every festival; six judges of these Olympic games retire and select the brightest compositions, which the respective successful acknowledge, kneel to Mrs Calliope, kiss her fair hand, and are crowned by it with myrtle … In short, since folly, which never ripens to madness but in this climate, ran distracted, there never was anything so entertaining, or so dull.

The standard of the verses penned at Batheaston can be judged from four volumes of Poetical Amusements at a Villa near Bath, edited by Lady Miller under a pseudonym which allowed her to indulge in lavish self-adulation. The proceeds from the sale of the books went to the Pauper Charity of Bath.

The parties – and the poems – came to an end when Lady Miller died in 1781. The rotunda has survived, but the vase has disappeared, giving rise to the belief that it found its way into Royal Victoria Park, where it can still be seen facing the path leading from Upper Church Street. Comparing a eighteenth-century illustration by W Hildare of the Batheaston Vase with the one in the park, however, it is clear they are not the same. The Batheaston Vase was much smaller and had leaves and floral patterns as well as bands of grooving running round it; the vase in the park has scenes of rustic life and a couple of serpents coiling themselves round the top. It is also solid, which would have made it impossible for anyone to place poems in it.

BATHFORD

Dominating the Bathford skyline, **Browne's Folly** (ST793662) is just over the parish boundary in Monkton Farleigh, and is therefore in Wiltshire. However, as it is commonly regarded as being in Bathford and is in a nature reserve administered by the Avon Wildlife Trust, it seems appropriate to include it here. Known locally as 'the Pepperpot', its style recalls the Tuscan towers on the Italianate mansions built by Henry Edmund Goodridge on Bathwick Hill in the mid-nineteenth century. Its position overlooking the Avon Valley was exploited in the Second World War for observation and surveying purposes when a tent was placed

Browne's Folly in the early twentieth century before the view was obscured by trees

on top by the Ordnance Survey. From the top of the tower, the Bristol Channel and Westbury White Horse can be seen on a clear day. Its lack of decoration and blind windows give it a forbidding look, somewhat alleviated by the design of the upper floor with its deep eaves, semi-circular-headed openings and balustraded handrails, parts of which are now missing.

On a tablet six metres up is inscribed:

W 1848 B

E

C 1907 H

WB was Mr Wade Browne, a quarry owner who bought Monkton Farleigh manor in 1842, and built the tower six years later (the E stands for 'erected'). CH was Charles Hobhouse, who acquired the estate in the early twentieth century and added the tablet in 1907. He used the tower as a luncheon rendezvous for shooting parties.

Like Blaine's Folly (qv) on the other side of Bath, the tower was probably built to relieve unemployment. Wade Browne was a noted philanthropist, who improved the road through Farleigh Wick, had water piped from Ash Well to a communal pump in Monkton Farleigh, donated a barrel organ to the church, and endowed a school where he also taught.

In the late twentieth century, the Avon Wildlife Trust acquired the land around the tower and in 1998 handed custody of the tower to the Folly Fellowship. Although lack of funds meant that full restoration and opening to the public could not be considered immediately, a new copper roof was added to the tower to prevent further deterioration.

BREWHAM

After creating the earthly paradise of Stourhead Garden, Henry Hoare 'the Magnificent' wrote to 'Sukey', his daughter Susanna, in 1762, saying that he had 'one scheme more which will crown or top all'. His words were well chosen, for **Alfred's Tower** (ST745351) was originally conceived to commemorate the accession of King George III in 1760 as well as the peace with France. However, he was so impressed by Alfred's exploits after reading Voltaire's L'Histoire Générale that he decided to erect the tower in his honour. Hoare hoped to find a 'quar of stone' to build the tower, but eventually settled for red brick instead. It was three years before construction began and another seven before it was complete, by which time the 49-metre-high tower had used up about a million bricks and cost nearly £6,000.

The designer was Henry Flitcroft who had worked on some of the temples at Stourhead. Hoare did not choose the landscaped grounds at Stourhead as the site for the tower, opting instead for Kingsettle Hill, which was close to where

Alfred's Tower

Alfred was reputed to have gathered together the men of Wiltshire, Hampshire and Somerset before defeating the Danes at Edington. The exact spot was St Egbert's Stone at Bourton just over the county border in Dorset, but this would have lacked the dramatic potential of Kingsettle, which, at 260 metres above sea level, was one of the highest points in the area. On a fine day it can be seen from as far away as Beckford's Tower on Lansdown (qv).

The triangular design of the tower, with circular turrets at each corner, has proved well able to withstand the strong winds. It is topped by conical pinnacles connected by crenellated parapets and between the turrets the tower is hollow and open to the sky. A staircase winds up one of the turrets to a viewing platform and a there is a statue of Alfred in a rustic Gothic style about nine metres up on the east side of the tower. Under it is this inscription:

ALFRED THE GREAT
AD 879 on this Summit
Erected his Standard
Against Danish Invaders
To him we owe the Origin of Juries
The Establishment of a Militia
The Creation of a Naval Force
Alfred the Light of a Benighted Age
Was a Philosopher and a Christian
The Father of his People
The Founder of the English
Monarchy and Liberty

In 1944 a plane crashed into the Tower. The five American airmen on board were killed but the Tower, although damaged, survived. When it was restored in 1986, a Wessex helicopter lowered a 300-kilogramme carved stone into place on the top. The architect Peter Bird worked from old pictures to produce a carving of four decorative leaves similar to the pinnacles on Wells Cathedral. St Blaise, the builders he worked with, considered that their main artistic achievement was the restoration of the statue of King Alfred.

The narrow cul-de-sac leading off the Upton Noble to North Brewham road passes closes to a Site of Special Scientific Interest, designated as such for its wildlife. However, **Cannwood Farm** is also a site of Special Folly Interest, for here entrepreneur Tony Garnett has developed an estate with a touch of individuality thanks to the most gifted of garden designers, Julian Bannerman, whose international reputation for modern and curious creations has led him to work for Jacob Rothschild, the Gettys and Prince Charles.

The Grotto at Cannwood Farm

On the main lawn of the house stands his wooden **Grotto** (ST739377), shaped a little like what one might expect a stone grotto to be, but with very few stones in it. Rather, it is mainly burr elm, a jumble of gnarled, twisted stumps, branches and roots, jutting out at crazy angles, but stabilised by several trunks growing out of the ground, to create one roughly round, irregular shape.

The entrance leads into a small dark chamber where visitors are greeted by the slightly frightening sight of the sculpture of a black wooden sheep, brought from Ireland. The floor is mainly of flint with ammonites set into it, and against one wall is a stove with a chimney where one could happily make tea on a sunny afternoon. This is the dark forest brought to the light of a Somerset garden – Andy Garnett calls it 'a poor man's foolishness, rather than a rich man's folly'.

BRIDGWATER

Although Castle House (ST299372) has often been described as an architectural monstrosity, this is rather missing the point, for like the 67-metre-high concrete tower at Sway in Hampshire, it was built not so much to please the eye as to demonstrate the qualities of a particular building material, in this case Portland cement. It is also innovative in its methods of reinforcement using brick, concrete and iron, making it a very early example of constructional post-tensioning.

It was built in 1851 by John Board (1802-1861), a local manufacturer and merchant of building materials, who exploited the blue lias limestone quarries at

Dunball on the River Parrett. For Castle House he experimented in making the cement, as well as pre-cast concrete facing panels and concrete blocks. Its basic form is rectangular, and it was built in three distinct sections, rear, middle and front. The front was the most ornate, and each of the three floors has a distinct external appearance. The ground floor is built mainly of brick with smooth concrete facing panels with gothic elements such as decorated drip-mouldings. A band of rusticated concrete blocks with a circular pattern separates it from the first floor, which is made entirely of concrete and is one of the first examples of load-bearing concrete in the world. A rusticated band with a different circular pattern separates the first and second floors. The second floor also consists of prominent blocks, and is topped by a parapet in the form of battlements, some of whose merlons bear classical cartouches.

There is a small attic under the gables which is only accessible by an external concrete spiral staircase, but may at one time have been connected internally with the first floor.

The façade is flanked by canted bays, each storey of which incorporates a niche. Most of these six niches are bare, but the right one on the first floor used to contain a painted statue of Napoleon, and the left one still contains a console supporting a carved head. A seventh niche in the bay in the centre of the ground floor, which is also empty, has drip-moulds terminating in small grotesque heads.

Castle House before the scaffolding went up

Despite its pioneering use of new materials, some ancient pieces of masonry also found their way into Castle House, perhaps as an ironic gesture of acknowledgement that, while the techniques used to build it were revolutionary, its style, like that of the buildings Brunel had designed for the railway through Bridgwater ten years earlier, was rooted in the past. The provenance of these fragments is unknown, but Bridgwater Castle, which used to stand nearby, is a likely source.

Today the building, hidden behind scaffolding and plastic sheeting, is in a parlous state. Now that its Grade II listing has been upgraded to Grade II*, on account of its groundbreaking building methods, it has become something of a cause célèbre, receiving nationwide coverage on the BBC's Restoration series. It has now been handed over to the SAVE Britain's Heritage Trust by Sedgemoor District Council.

BRISLINGTON

On the approach to Bristol along the Bath Road stand two remarkable buildings, the first a light-coloured stone **Gateway** (ST612717) with statues in niches and, behind it, the medieval-looking **Black Castle**. They were both built by William Reeve, an eighteenth-century merchant who made a fortune smelting zinc, copper and brass, and whose works were a short distance away at Crew's Hole on the River Avon. Reeve also built Arno's Court, on the other side of the Bath Road. This elegant house with Rococo and Gothic touches, which was originally connected to the Black Castle by a tunnel, is now a hotel.

Little is known of Reeve except that he was Master of the Merchant Venturers in 1765 and went bankrupt nine years later. He probably decided to call this area Arno's Vale because of an affinity – real or imagined – to the countryside around Florence, through which the River Arno runs. Although it is difficult to find any point of comparison today, as late as 1911, when the Black Castle was put up for sale, the auction catalogue claimed that it was 'the Replica of a Castle on the Banks of the River Arno in Italy'.

The truth is somewhat more prosaic. Reeve used the slag created during the smelting process to make black blocks with which he built the castle. Also known as Arno's Castle, the building contained stables, offices and a banqueting room. Like Ralph Allen's Prior Park, it was probably also intended to demonstrate the uses to which this unconventional building material, which he was producing large quantities of as a by-product of his metal-making business, could be put.

The courtyard of the Black Castle in the early twentieth century

Not everyone was impressed. Horace Walpole called it a 'large gothic building, coal black and striped with white. I took it for the Devil's Cathedral'. Its blackness is relieved by pale freestone dressings in the form of crenellations, Gothic tracery and ornamental tablets and shields. There are two large square towers, each about 10 metres high. The one at the east end has a blank panel which may once have borne the royal coat of arms. The western tower presides over the courtyard, and has an empty niche which once contained a carved figure, believed to have been an alderman at prayer, above a finely carved head of Henry VIII. Lower down is a coat of arms which may be that of Reeve. There are circular towers at each of the four corners, and two intermediate turrets half way between the square tower on the west and the corner towers. A chapel on the first floor of the west tower is said to be haunted by a nun who was ravished and killed close to the Black Castle; a woman claims to have seen and talked to her in a ladies' toilet in 1988.

Some internal decoration has survived, including bosses in the form of grotesque heads. However, the Black Castle has undergone several makeovers; in 2005 it was fitted out as a bar with minimalist décor and large television screens.

The architect of the Black Castle is unknown, although if the date of 1764, which appears on a stone on the east tower, is to be believed, it may have been James Bridges, who rebuilt St Werburgh's Church in 1758-61. The gothic windows and freestone may have come from the old church after demolition. However, Tim Mowl suggests William and John Halfpenny as more likely candidates because of the incidence of towers and turrets in their pattern books.

The Black Castle as it appears from the road today

Before the Black Castle was engulfed by urban sprawl, it had a garden with a fishpond on the south side, at the end of which was a **Bath House**. This was built around the same time as the castle and was a place for Reeve's workers to relax. In total contrast to the castle, it had 14 Corinthian columns, some of which supported three stone vases on a parapet, as well as two small side pavilions, each with an onion-shaped dome. It is not known when it ceased to be used as a bath house, but by the 1920s Messrs Little & Barber were displaying antique furniture on a floor built over the pool. Their advertisements extolled the virtues of this unique showroom in lavish terms:

> The interior does not belie the promise of the exterior and is of elongated shape, the ceiling of which is enriched with Chippendale designs, in the one case depicting a castle amid rural surroundings, and in the other a similar scene with goats browsing in the foreground. The minor enrichments of the ceiling are emblematic of water fountains, dolphins etc, whilst a pretty cornice runs round the apartment excised with acanthus leaves, below which are a series of metallic heads, conjectured to be likenesses of William Reeve and his daughter. Around the walls are seven niches doubtless originally filled with statuary. On entering the visitor will not fail to be struck with the architectural beauty of the main doorway. On either side of this interesting apartment are ante or dressing rooms, the friezes of which are decorated with the fruit of the pineapple. Special note should be made of the right-hand ante-room which contains a fireplace of Gothic design and three quaintly framed mirrors.

The interior of the Bath House at the Black Castle in the early twentieth century

Tragically the Bath House is no more, except for the colonnade which was rescued by Clough Williams-Ellis for his home for retired follies at Portmeirion in North Wales. Some of the plasterwork, by Thomas Paty, was moved to the City Museum and Art Gallery.

Around 1766, Reeve commissioned James Bridges or William Paty (or possibly both) to build an imposing gateway for Arno's Court. Built, like the Court, of Bath stone, and about nine metres high, it is classically proportioned but covered with Gothic and Moorish decorations. Statues from two of Bristol's demolished city gates once filled the niches, giving rise to the erroneous belief that the entire gate had been moved here from somewhere else and dated back to medieval times. After standing empty for many years, the niches are once again occupied by Bath stone replicas, the ones at the front being Edward I on the right and Edward III on the left, while those at the back are probably of the three Magi.

Above, the Gateway at Arnos Vale in the early twentieth century, still surrounded by fields; below, the Gateway today

In 1912 the gateway was moved to its present site to make way for road widening. In the 1990s, a further road was built along its western side, and, along with the Black Castle, it is now surrounded by the trappings of modern life, including a large supermarket.

BROMPTON REGIS

The forlorn-looking and rather plain **Louisa Gate Tower** (SS937287) is something of an enigma. It is a circular, roofless building with an arched doorway leading into it and a tiny opening near the top. There is no evidence, such as holes for supporting pieces of wood, of a stairway, but signs suggest there may

have been a walkway around the parapet. The render that once covered the rubble sandstone has, like the crenellations, crumbled away over the years.

Although it may have been built as a hunting lodge or observation tower, its modest proportions suggest that it is more likely to have been some sort of shelter, with crenellations added to make it an eyecatcher from Pixton Park on the other side of the valley.

It is tempting to suppose that it was named after a lady called Louisa who lived at Pixton Park. A more likely explanation, however, is that Louisa is a corruption of 'looze' or 'lews', West Somerset names for a pigsty. Its appearance as 'lousy gate' in a document of 1759 reinforces this theory. Its proximity to Swine's Cleeve Wood also supports this rather mundane explanation of why it was built. It would have been well placed in autumn, when pigs were turned loose in the wood to feed on acorns or beechmast – a custom known as pannage.

BROOMFIELD

The **Folly** (ST222322) at **Fyne Court** may look an innocuous little fancy but it once formed part of the scene of some unusual goings-on, sometimes exaggerated by those hostile to the experiments of the owner, Andrew Crosse (1784-1855). This intelligent and hospitable country squire became known as the Wizard of the Quantocks for his experiments with electricity. As early as 1816 he was predicting that electricity would enable people to communicate instantaneously 'with the uttermost parts of the earth' and would be 'employed in a vast variety of manufactures throughout the world'. Although condemned as 'a reviler of our Holy Religion', a number of eminent scientists, including Sir Humphrey Davy, the President of the Royal Society and a pioneer of electro-chemistry, visited him at Fyne Court. Another visitor was Ada Lovelace from Ashley Combe (qv) at Porlock. Although she recognised Crosse's intellect and enthusiasm, she condemned his 'lack of system' and failure to commit his findings to paper.

We do not know whether Crosse conducted any experiments in the Folly. The nerve centre of operations was some distance away, in the Music Room, a detached building which survived the destruction of the main house by fire in

The Folly at Fyne Court

Front and back views of the Boathouse at Fyne Court

1894. The Folly is said at one time to have been used as a prison and later as a kennel for the estate dogs. Built of rubble sandstone, originally covered in render and now partially covered in ivy, it consists of two low round crenellated towers separated by a coupling wall. The building is about 15 metres wide, with each tower about four metres wide and six metres high.

On an embankment above the folly, an ornamental canal runs along to a **Boathouse**, built, like the folly, of rubble stone and probably also covered in render at one time. The side facing the canal is reminiscent of the mausoleum at Hestercombe (qv), with a triangular pediment above a semi-circular brick arch; the other side is embattled with a gothic window.

BRYMPTON D'EVERCY

Nearly every country house has some quality about it whether of architecture, sentiment, historical associations or scenery, that makes it in the narrow sense of the word, incomparable. But Brympton has them all and unites them so perfectly that the whole cannot be surpassed, scarcely be analysed.

Christopher Hussey

A little to the west of Yeovil lies the ancient estate of **Brympton d'Evercy** (ST521154). Its name derives from the Norman family of d'Evercy who lived at Brympton in the thirteenth and fourteenth centuries. In 1325, it was described as a 'capital messuage with gardens and closes adjoining worth five shillings a year'. It was probably the Sydenhams, who lived here from the fifteenth to the seventeenth centuries, who built the earliest part of the **Clock Tower**, although not on the present site.

The Clock Tower at Brympton House

The Sydenhams enjoyed flaunting their wealth, and proceeded to knock down bits of the house and build new wings, but were eventually forced to dispose of the property due to debts. They could not find a buyer and had to mortgage the house to Thomas Penny, the Receiver General of Somerset. When Thomas Penny built the present, very ornate, porch on the west side of the house in 1722, he moved the original porch to the north side of the forecourt garden. The old porch formed the base for the Clock Tower which was completed in 1723, and has the form of an square archway. When the porch was originally built is uncertain – Pevsner suggests the sixteenth century – although the bellcote is likely to have been early seventeenth century. It is unlikely that it was part of the original porch because it would not have fitted in with the west façade of the house and would have obstructed the upstairs windows. In any case there is a clear break between the entablature above the arch and the upper part of the tower. Furthermore, an early eighteenth-century view of the estate by Knyff (who can usually be relied upon for accuracy) shows only a small porch on the west front and no tower.

The crest carved into the façade above the entablature is upside-down, though this is not obvious from its quatrefoil pattern. Less than a metre further up is a fine clock with numerals set into the Ham stone, which is said to be the oldest working clock in the West Country. The bellcote, with a pyramidal roof, four openings to front and back, and one on each side, is at the back.

When the town hall in Yeovil burnt down in 1935, Violet Clive, the owner of Brympton, rescued some of the material before it was demolished to adorn her garden. It is from this period that the **Corinthian Temple** at the end of the south terrace dates. With four Corinthian columns, a plain entablature and pediment, it now houses an old rustic cart which is almost too big for it. The Japanese stone lantern that

The Corinthian Temple at Brympton House - complete with cart

stands on an island in the lake comes not from Yeovil, however, but from Kyoto, where Mrs Clive's brother, Richard Ponsonby-Fane, spent much of his life.

BUTLEIGH

Vice Admiral Sir Samuel Hood (1762-1814), the grandson of the eldest brother of the Vicar of Butleigh, was a prominent naval officer who served alongside Wellington and distinguished himself in embarking the troops at Corunna. Like the Iron Duke, he is commemorated by a very tall monument, in his case at Windmill Hill, in that part of Butleigh Wood which lies in the parish of Dundon. The **Hood Monument** (ST495338) was designed in 1831 by Bath architect Henry Edmund Goodridge, who also built Beckford's Tower (qv). Despite being surrounded by trees, it enjoys fine views of the countryside punctuated to the north by Glastonbury Tor.

Samuel Hood was one of several members of his family who enjoyed distinguished naval careers, others of whom were also called Samuel. He should not be confused with his father's cousin, Samuel, Admiral Lord Hood, whose son, the 2nd Baron Bridport, inherited the estate at Cricket St Thomas (qv). As one of Nelson's 'Band of Brothers', the Samuel commemorated at Butleigh was affectionately known as Sam, and distinguished himself throughout the Napoleonic

Wars, notably at the Battles of the Nile, Algeciras and Trafalgar. He was so tall that when he commanded the Weasel brig he had to put his head through the skylight so that the barber could dress his hair on deck. He had an easy-going manner, a lack of affectation and a gentleness that was reflected in his eyes and the humorous curve of his mouth. Unlike Nelson, he learned the language of the enemy by spending two years in France during the peace in the 1790s, thereby gaining a better understanding of Napoleon's people. He enjoyed great respect from his men; when, after losing his right arm in action, his crew watched him

The Hood Monument

being lowered over the side of his ship at Ryde, 'you would have really thought', an eye-witness observed, 'that every man in the ship was his brother'.

In his monument we have a structure which elevates column building to the highest level of artistic merit. While the base of the column is fairly straightforward and the Tuscan column has perhaps too much entasis, or curving, in its shaft, the top is a superb sculpture on a nautical theme. Drum-shaped, it has laurel wreaths at the four points of the compass, each pierced by a circular opening, surmounted by a naval crown – the sterns of four galleons interspersed with four mainsails. Pevsner records that there was once a glass dome, but there is no trace of it now, and the monument is topped by a plain ball finial. It is difficult to appreciate the details of the lavish decoration without some kind of optical magnification, however, as it is 33 metres above ground level.

There is no such problem with viewing the base, on three of whose sides are laudatory and patriotic inscriptions. On the north face is inscribed:

IN MEMORY OF
SIR SAMUEL HOOD
BARONET
KNIGHT OF THE MOST HONOURABLE ORDER OF THE BATH
AND NOMINATED GRAND CROSS THEREOF
KNIGHT OF ST FERDINAND AND OF MERIT
KNIGHT GRAND CROSS OF THE SWORD
VICE ADMIRAL OF THE WHITE
AND COMMANDER IN CHIEF OF HIS MAJESTY'S FLEET
IN THE EAST INDIES

The White refers to one of the three squadrons of His Majesty's Fleet, the others being the Blue and the Red. Although the system was obsolete by this time, Red, White and Blue were retained as rank titles. The west face reads:

AN OFFICER OF THE HIGHEST DISTINCTION
AMONGST THE ILLUSTRIOUS MEN
WHO RENDERED THEIR OWN AGE
THE BRIGHTEST PERIOD
IN THE NAVAL HISTORY
OF THEIR COUNTRY

The epitaph concludes on the south face:

THIS MONUMENT IS DEDICATED
TO THEIR LATE COMMANDER
BY THE ATTACHMENT AND REVERENCE OF BRITISH OFFICERS
OF WHOM MANY WERE
HIS ADMIRING FOLLOWERS
IN THOSE AWFUL SCENES OF WAR
IN WHICH WHILE THEY CALL FORTH
THE GRANDEST QUALITIES OF HUMAN NATURE
IN HIM LIKEWISE GAVE OCCASION
FOR THE EXERCISE OF ITS MOST AMIABLE VIRTUES
HE DIED AT MADRAS DECEMBER 24TH 1814

CHAFFCOMBE

Avishays House, two miles east of Chard, dates from the seventeenth century, but was substantially rebuilt between 1745 and 1759. A park was also laid out around the house at the same time. The estate belonged to the same family (the Sealys and later, by marriage, the Marwoods) from 1697 to 1859, when it was sold to a Chard solicitor called Edward Clarke.

It is likely that the **Monmouth Tower** (ST354092), also known as the Castle, was built during Clarke's ownership as he would have had the money for such fancies, the previous owner, Reverend George Notley, having been insane for 30 years before his death in 1857. It stands on Whitemoor Hill to the east of the house, on the site of a sham castle which had fallen into ruins. A square single-storey building of rubble stone with some flintwork and Ham stone dressings, it served as a water tower as well as an eyecatcher from the house. There is a simple doorway on the west side, and windows on the north and south. An embattled parapet runs round the top of the walls and a leaded, bell-hipped roof rises to a wooden turret, recessed in the corners, with a hipped roof and ball finial. A clock on the west side faces the house; its hand-wound clock mechanism dates from 1873, although the clock face may be twentieth century. It was made by Gillet & Johnson of Croydon who also created an attractive and rather unusual chime.

The Monmouth Tower at Avishays

Built into the side of Whitemoor Hill is a former **Ice House** which may date from the eighteenth century. It is octagonal in plan, has a slate roof with ball finial and two high walls stretching either side of the white door which opens into a cruciform chamber with arched niches.

The Monmouth Tower derives its name from the narrow escape experienced by Elias Sealy who owned Avishays in 1685 when the Duke of Monmouth landed his troops at nearby Lyme Regis and laid claim to the English throne. The rebellion failed, and troops loyal to James II scoured the region for his supporters, who included Mr Sealy. He was informed just in time that he was about to be arrested, and so he hid in a tree in his grounds. The officers could not find him in the house, so they searched the grounds. As they approached the tree, an owl flew out, and for some reason they concluded that Mr Sealy was not there. Thus they left the estate empty-handed, and for many years servants of the Sealys were instructed not to harm owls as the bird had saved the family. A building in the grounds was even used as an owlery for them to nest in.

The whole structure is in a very good state of repair; it is possible that the wooden turret is not an original feature but was added at a later date, perhaps when the building ceased to be used to supply water to the house, but in the absence of documentary evidence this must remain conjecture. What is beyond question is that this beautifully proportioned but very unusual building, tucked away in the high hills of South Somerset, far from a main road, is one of the most engaging follies in the county.

CHANTRY

Somerset, like other parts of the country, has seen shifts in population as traditional industries have declined, leaving former hives of activity deserted. One area that suffered a sharp decline lies along the Mells River near Frome where the ironworks of the Fussell family once flourished. The Fussells, who produced and exported agricultural implements, were part of a long tradition of Mendip ironmaking. At one time the now peaceful, honey-stoned village of Mells was known as Iron Burgh, such was the importance of the industry. The house called the Chantry was built about 1825 by James Fussell V (1774-1845), and it is likely that the **Grotto** (ST719466) came a little later, probably about 1830, as part of a landscape scheme designed to embellish a lake which had been dammed to supply power to the ironworks about a mile away.

Today, all is silence around the grotto, buried deep in woods, and its labyrinthine nature and extent strikes wonder into the beholder At its highest point, there are four 'access' towers, consisting of arches joined together. At the sides, there appear to have been various collapses, with the remains of a row of niches along a balcony. There is a local legend that these were once used for opium smoking. Several narrow staircases lead down to a pool, from which a stream issues, and small boulders are scattered everywhere. To one side is a high circular court with a hole in the roof and five niches with seats.

From the court a dark tunnel weaved its way towards a blocked entrance, behind which, according to Robin Atthill in Old Mendip, was once a grindstone. He also recorded an ice-house, consisting of a deep stone-lined pit, a short distance away on the north-facing hillside. Back towards the lower lake, there is a separate, squarish cascade on one side, as well as a bridge with rock arches in four parts. The whole scene is very sylvan, with substantial yew-tree cover, extensive moss, and a luxuriant growth of ferns. A somewhat dilapidated scene, but one to treasure.

CHEWTON KEYNSHAM

Perhaps the most unusual and intriguing tower in the county can be found in the grounds of a conference centre south of Keynsham. This is the **Owl Hoot** (ST656669) at Chewton Place – or the 'wolery', as locals, with more than a nod to AA Milne, prefer to call it. Vaguely reminiscent of a disused, and now slightly askew, lime kiln, this buttressed, four-square structure, tapering to a pyramidal top, stands about nine metres high. Built of pale grey rubble stone, it appears to consist of five storeys, with holes (some now blocked up) in the four upper ones for owls to roost in. An archway leads through the tower at ground level. Over the keystone of one entrance is the figure of an owl, while the keystone on the other side is blank.

The Owl Hoot at Chewton Place; below, the owl over the entrance

The fascination with animals continues on the colonnade, added to the Georgian house nearby in the nineteenth century, with bears, rabbits and foxes set in cartouches. The identity of the owl fancier whose folly graces this charming garden on the banks of the River Chew is unknown. One candidate is Thomas Lediard who bought the estate in 1766 and built the house. He was a dry salter who used Chewton Keynsham mill for his logwood business. He is the least likely, however, for in 1786, shortly after building the house, he advertised it to let. Another candidate is either Philip Jones, a business partner of Thomas Lediard's son, or Philip Jones's wife's grandson. Records for the early nineteenth century are somewhat confusing, but it seems that one of them added the façade to the house and made other improvements to the estate. The most likely candidate, however, is Henry Eden Mynors, who owned the estate later in the nineteenth century, the period when, according to a survey by the Institute of Advanced Architectural Studies, the Owl Hoot is likely to have been built.

CHILTON POLDEN

High on Cock Hill, part of the long ridge of the Polden Hills which runs eastward from Bridgwater towards the Hood Monument near Butleigh, stands the repository of some of Somerset's finest architectural and archaeological fragments. This is the so-called **Chilton Priory** (ST374389), otherwise known as Stradling's Folly. It was built in the 1830s by William Stradling, an antiquarian and collector who salvaged pieces of buildings and archaeological relics from around the county and assembled them here. Standing at the entrance, a visitor to the Priory sees a tower and a long wall. There is little to indicate the extraordinary castellated house that lies behind it.

Chilton Priory in the early twentieth century

In 1839, Stradling published a Description of the Priory of Chilton-Super-Polden and its Contents, making it clear that his efforts had not met with universal approval:

> A remark is made by every passer-by, and he is called to account in every quarter for having dared to obtrude anything so ugly, unmeaning, ill-proportioned, yet still so conspicuous, on the omnipotent eye of the public.

In his defence, Stradling pointed out that the Priory was 'intended rather as a pleasing object at a distance, being placed on very high ground, than as a specimen of architecture'. Addressing the criticism that the tower was out of proportion, he argued that, 'if the Tower had been built in proportion to its height, the rooms would have been so very small as to be perfectly useless, and as the doors, windows etc were taken from other buildings, no regular proportion could be observed; and nothing could be done to arrange the whole so as to be as little irksome as possible to the eye of the connoisseur'.

Stradling did, however, make some attempt at ecclesiastical authenticity in the Priory, incorporating features customary in churches or monasteries, albeit not necessarily in their customary positions. There is a nave, an oratory, an embattled tower, a crypt, and an ambulatory in the inner courtyard. Many of the fragments used to build the Priory came from the area around Chedzoy, where Stradling excavated numerous relics including pottery, a hypocaust, and iron slag from a Roman villa, as well as buttresses and Gothic tracery from a house once owned by the church. The tracery was installed in the west tower, whose upper windows, battlements and grotesque heads came from a demolished castle at Enmore. Pinnacles came from the old church tower at Langport, the staircase turret from a church in Shepton Mallet, and three of the windows in the nave from a chapel at Slapeland. The cross and finial from Chedzoy parish church, thrown down by Cromwell's soldiers, found a new home on a gable end, although they have since disappeared.

In autumn the inner courtyard is brightened by reddening virginia creeper which obscures some of the features on the west side. There is no problem, however, making out a round-arched ambulatory on the south side, and a font near the main door of the courtyard. From here, steps lead up to a parapet-cum-balcony overlooking the road, with a sculpture of two mythological animals.

Stradling was fascinated not only by old buildings but also by old legends.

Inside Pococks's Cell

One concerned a 'most extraordinary character' called Pocock who had lived in a cave about a quarter of a mile away. In a gully in the western part of the Priory garden, Stradling created **Pocock's Cell** in an attempt to recreate the atmosphere of the original cave. It is approached by a narrow path between high banks, crossed at one point by a bridge, and screened by dense undergrowth. The cell is a simple square chamber with a doorless opening, three pointed niches on the back wall and a small opening in the ceiling to let light through. It is said to have once contained the marble statue of a reclining woman, but, if so, it has gone. Further along the path is a pond with a two-arched back wall. A metre-high gothic pinnacle, no doubt salvaged from another church, stands nearby. Stradling also apparently built a free-standing tower in an adjacent field, but this too has disappeared.

Stradling does not seem to have lived in the Priory for very long. In his book, he refers to a 'Gothic Cottage' with curious oak carvings by William Halliday, 'the present occupier of the Priory'. It is believed that Halliday oversaw the building of the Priory, although the name of John Westlake Wainwright has also been mentioned in this regard.

CLAVERTON

Once attributed to Sir Jeffry Wyatville, it is now known that **Claverton Manor** (ST784642) was built by John Vivian, the son of the original owner, around 1820. His lack of experience had at least one unfortunate consequence – he failed to include a kitchen! Now home to the American Museum in Britain, its Italianate grounds contain two nineteenth-century vernacular buildings – a native Cheyenne tepee and a **Milliner's Shop**, housed in a Dutch summer house. The grounds also include a garden inspired by George Washington's garden at Mount Vernon in Virginia, with a replica of the octagonal schoolroom where he taught his step-grandchildren.

A hundred metres or so from the house, facing the lawn, is a Niche, built from rubble and flint, with an ashlar arch, set into a short four-metre-high wall. It has

The Grotto at Claverton Manor

a fairly grand but plain cornice, a course of stones running above it and another running through it, with a carved shell inset above. Water pours from a spout in a lion's head into a pool below. It is sometimes referred to as a **Grotto**, but, like Delia's Grotto in Bath (qv), it is a rather truncated one. Neither its date nor maker are known, but its style suggests that it was built around the same time as the house.

CLEVEDON

Clevedon Court (ST423716) was built by Sir John de Clevedon around 1320 and is one of the oldest manor houses in Somerset. In 1630, the Wake family acquired the estate, and in 1709 it was bought by a wealthy Bristol merchant called Sir Abraham Elton. His son, also called Abraham (1679-1742), became Sheriff and Mayor of Bristol, as well as Master of the Merchant Venturers. He

The Turret, Octagon and Shelter at Clevedon Court

not only remodelled the court but laid out terraces running up the hillside behind it, incorporating part of a building dating from the twelfth or thirteenth century. This is a crenellated **Turret**, which once formed part of the kitchen and domestic office range, and is linked to the court by a crenellated rubble wall. Standing about four metres high, it consists of a single round room with small windows. A lean-to gothic-style extension was added to it in the nineteenth century.

At the west end of the higher terrace is the **Octagon**, a creeper-covered building with colour-washed walls, sash windows on the south side, a cornice and parapet and a pyramidal roof with a ball finial at its apex, built by Sir Abraham Elton IV (1718-90). Facing it, at the east end of the terrace, is an open-fronted, rubble-stone **Shelter**, with an ashlar archway, above which the wall sweeps up to a ball finial. A lower extension on the south side, possibly added at a later date, has a gothic archway leading to another part of the grounds.

An early view of Clevedon Court showing Wake's Tower on the hill above

Court Hill, which rises above the terraces, was a bare tract of land until Sir Abraham Elton V planted it with exotic trees in the 1820s. A painting by an unknown artist which hangs in the court shows it before the trees were planted, with a large folly-type building dominating the scene. This was **Wake's Tower**, which, if the painting is accurate, had a tall archway and four short, spiky finials. Possibly built as a watchtower at the time of the Spanish Armada, according to Collinson it was demolished sometime before 1738. A summerhouse was built on the site but this too was in ruins by the early nineteenth century.

COMBE FLOREY

One of the chief landmarks in this part of the Quantocks, **Winter's Tower** (ST141317) was built by John Winter of Watts House in 1790. The tower served several purposes. First, it was an eyecatcher from Watts House, a mile and a half away. Second, it provided a home for Winter's gamekeeper, although, with five storeys, it is unlikely that he used all the accommodation available. Third,

Winter's Tower

and perhaps most crucially, it allowed Winter to spy on his neighbours, the Lethbridges of Sandhill Park, with whom he had lengthy – and extremely costly – legal battles.

Although the Lethbridges' opinion of the tower is not recorded, Edward Jeboult, who wrote A General Account of West Somerset in 1873, was distinctly underwhelmed. 'The view from the summit is not extensive, being almost confined to the surrounding parishes', he wrote, adding that the tower was 'a very debased attempt to represent a church tower'. There is, however, no evidence that Winter intended his tower to look like that of a church. Indeed, with its numerous windows – three on each floor, front and back – and a short wing, set slightly back, it is, despite many of the windows being in the gothic style, more reminiscent of an industrial than an ecclesiastical building.

In 1991, Des Baker, a builder from Burnham on Sea, restored the tower, replacing the render which had originally covered its sandstone walls, and installing modern conveniences.

COTHELSTONE

When Edward Esdaile built Cothelstone House in 1818 he created a lake in which its Ionic portico would be reflected. Mr Lane, the estate carpenter, also built a summerhouse and a rustic arbour with a thatched roof in the grounds. Just under a mile to the east, 323 metres up on Cothelstone Hill, a nine-metre high **Tower** (ST189326), was built of rubble stone. A 360-page journal, written by an estate worker in the mid-nineteenth century, has been preserved in the Somerset

Cothelstone Tower as it appeared in the early twentieth century

Record Office. Hidden among the financial accounts, rabbit coursing records, and tips on estate management is the throwaway comment: 'Summerhouse on the summit of Cliff-field was built 1832'. A few pages further on, however, the writer returns to the subject of the tower, stating that 'nothing is known when this was first erected. From it, however, on a clear day a magnificent view is obtained – it is said the most extensive in England'.

It was a popular rendezvous on high days and holidays. Even Edward Jeboult, normally scornful of such frivolities, admitted that 'it is a favourite

place for picnics. The sides and slopes of the hill, especially towards the west, are beautifully studded with trees, especially beech.' It commanded a view of the Wellington Monument, while about a mile away, just off the road to West Bagborough, there used to stand a curious statue on a rubble-stone plinth with a niche containing a seat. Some 300 metres down the slope are the ruins of a squarish building which might also have acted as an eyecatcher from Cothelstone House, but we do not know its purpose. The poet Edward Thomas rested here at the end of a bicycle journey from London to the Quantocks in the spring of 1913 and recorded the following impressions:

> I saw through the trees the grey mass of Cothelstone Manor beside its lake, and twelve miles off the Wellington obelisk on the Blackdown Hills. A stone seat on the other side of the trees commands both the manor house beneath and the distant obelisk. The seat is in an arched-over recess in the thickness of a square wall of masonry, six or seven feet in height and breadth. A coeval old hawthorn, spare and solitary, sticks out from the base of the wall. The whole is surmounted by a classic stone statue of an emasculated man larger than human, nude except for some drapery falling behind, long-haired, with left arm uplifted, and under its feet a dog; and it looks straight over at the obelisk. I do not know if the statue and the obelisk are connected, nor, if so, whether the statue represents the Iron Duke, his king, or a classic deity … The statue and masonry, darkened and bitten by the weather in that high, remote, commanding place, has in any case long outgrown the original conception and intention, and become a classi-rustical, romantic what-you-please, waiting for its poet or prose poet. I should have liked very well, on such a day, in such a position, to think it a Somerset Pan or Apollo, but could not. It was mainly pathetic and partly ridiculous.

Today it is more pathetic still, for in the 1990s it was toppled from its lofty eminence and now lies forlornly on the hillside. The tower has also succumbed to the elements and is now no more than a heap of stones; the house from which it formed an eyecatcher was demolished in 1962.

Sic transit gloria mundi

CRANMORE

According to Mary de Viggiani, who has chronicled Cranmore's history, in the 1860s

> a fashion had grown up among the landed gentry to build themselves folly towers to view the surrounding countryside. Those whose estates stretched over a suitable mileage could boast that they could oversee their property more conveniently. Locally several of the gentry had laid bets as to which of them could build the highest tower. This wager was won by a tower built of wood by a neighbouring landowner; however this tower did not survive and can no longer be admired.

One tower that has survived is the 45-metre-high **Cranmore Tower** (ST677450), built by John Moore Paget in 1862-4. Designed by Thomas Wyatt, who had already extended Cranmore Hall for Paget, its construction was overseen by William Witcombe of Leigh-on-Mendip. To ensure that it was the talk of the

Cranmore Tower

neighbourhood, a lavish 'roof raising dinner', lasting over six hours, was held at the manor when the roof of the tower was finally installed.

The tower was built to restore a view lost amid fir plantations. Reminiscent of a Tuscan look-out tower, the dark-coloured stone used to construct it came from a nearby quarry at Funtle. Viewing platforms, accessible from an internal timber staircase, were provided halfway up and at the top. Their iron railings were made by Samson Lintern & Sons of the Dean Smithy. The pyramidal roof, with overhanging eaves, has a ball finial at its apex.

Standing over 300 metres above sea level, it is said that you can see five counties from the top of the tower. In the Second World War, it was used by the Home Guard and the Royal Corps of Signals. By 1984, when Donald Beaton, a dairy farmer from Wincanton, bought it from Sir John Paget, the task of restoring it was so formidable that it acquired, in some quarters, the nickname Beaton's Folly. When he called in a diviner to find a source of water for the tower and for the cottage at its foot, he struck not water but the remains of a Roman fort with a massive hoard of coins. He also discovered lead pipes which had supplied the fort with water and tunnels to carry away sewage, neither of which, unfortunately, could be restored to their original purpose.

Despite the enormity of the task facing him, Donald Beaton ploughed ahead with the restoration. In 1988, he sold the tower to Nick Ridge, who opened it to the public with a range of attractions, including a forest craft walk, a children's adventure course, horse and pony rides, and a café. Since then, however, the tower has been acquired by a religious organisation and is no longer open to the public on a regular basis.

CREWKERNE

The **Gazebo** (ST443099) at Merefield House on East Street is a delightful example of that often-found ornament to the urban or village garden – the gazebo or summerhouse. The gazebo at Merefield House is built into a wall and commands a view over the terraces and steps leading up to it. Probably dating from the 1720s, it was built by John Merefield, lord of the manor of nearby Woolmington, who built the house in East Street as his town house. It was restored in the late twentieth century by St Blaise, the period building specialists from Dorchester.

Constructed of brick, the front of the gazebo is covered with stucco. Its most striking feature is a Dutch gable with an undulating moulded coping, which supports an eagle – once gilded – at the apex, and has a sundial in its centre. The gable rests on a moulded cornice supported by four pilasters, framing a

The Gazebo at Merefield House

pair of sash windows in moulded architraves with segmental arches and keystones, and a door over which is a moulded hood with a concave front. The interior, which has survived virtually intact, has a coved ceiling with a dome in the centre decorated with plasterwork vines; the walls have full-height panelling ending in a box cornice. A limestone fireplace has an eared architrave with stone hobs; niches, painted indigo with white shell reliefs, on either side of it, form a striking contrast with the terracotta painted walls.

CRICKET ST THOMAS

Cricket House (ST374085), described by Collinson as 'a very neat seat with elegant plantations, embellishing a spot by nature pleasing, and charmingly romantick', was acquired by Sir Alexander Hood, the 2nd Lord Bridport, in 1775. Eleven years later, he retired to the estate after a distinguished naval career and engaged Sir John Soane to demolish the house and build a new one on the site.

Fragments from the old house seem to have found their way into the **Admiral's Seat**, a Tudor-looking folly 650 metres to the north. The materials used are a pleasing mixture of Ham stone ashlar dressings around squared flint, with alternate stones boasted and recessed. At the corners are hexagonal pilasters with hollowed faces, and the roof is of slate. The front has a slightly cambered arched doorway, and above is a three-lighted window, blind except for a small circular opening in the central light. External ironwork suggests the lights may once have been open. Above the window is a datestone of 1595, almost certainly from the old house, while another stone, with the inscription 'erected 1795', indicates that the folly was built to commemorate the bicentenary of the house Howe demolished.

Now backed by mature trees, the Admiral's Seat commands extensive views over the valley of the River Axe. It is said that, from here, Lord Howe kept watch

The Admiral's Seat

with a spyglass over the fleet in Lyme Bay. Another legend has it that Nelson courted Lady Hamilton here. What is beyond conjecture is that when Lord Howe's great nephew, Samuel Hood, married Nelson's niece, Charlotte, he brought the title of the Duke of Bronte, which had been bestowed on Nelson by Ferdinand, King of the Two Sicilies, to the family. Samuel, who also inherited Lord Howe's estate and title, continued his great-uncle's work at Cricket St Thomas, damming a river to create a series of lakes, and destroying the village of Cricket St Thomas in the process. In the late nineteenth century, the estate was acquired by Francis Fry, the chocolate manufacturer. In the 1960s a wildlife park opened in the grounds; more recently the house was converted to a hotel and spa.

CROWCOMBE

In 1725, Thomas Carew, MP for Minehead, decided to demolish **Crowcombe Manor**, his ancestral home, and build a Palladian mansion a little further down the hill. Thomas Parker, the first architect he brought in, was fired after stealing a pot of money from the old hall and Nathaniel Ireson was brought in to finish the job. When the estate was sold after Carew's death in 1766, James Bernard, the new owner, replaced the formal terraces which Ireson had laid out around the house with a landscaped garden in the latest style. In the combe to the north of the house, he installed a succession of weirs to create cascades and built a rustic bridge across the stream. Dorothy Wordsworth, who visited Crowcombe whilst living nearby at Alfoxden, was somewhat critical of Bernard's attempts to improve on nature but still found the valley 'romantic and beautiful'. Whether she was influenced in her judgement by the presence of a ruined chapel high above the combe is, however, unknown.

Cardinal Beaufort's Chapel

Unlike most ruinous eyecatchers, **Cardinal Beaufort's Chapel** (ST142375), as it was known, started life as a genuine chapel, attached to Halsway Manor, a fifteenth-century manor house two miles to the north-west. It seems likely that, when he moved it, Bernard took the opportunity of redesigning the chapel to make it conform more closely to picturesque ideals. He may even have incorporated material from the old manor house at Crowcombe. The original chapel stood on the north-east side of Halsway Manor and dated from the time of Sir Edward Stradling, who inherited the estate in 1407. He married Joan, the natural daughter of Henry Beaufort, Cardinal Bishop of Winchester, who was a close advisor to his nephew, Henry V. Beaufort financed Henry's French campaigns, and sat on the tribunal which condemned Joan of Arc to burn at the stake.

The relocated chapel, which is cruciform in shape, stands two storeys high, although any upper floors have long since disappeared. Built of red sandstone with limestone dressings, it has the Gothic look which features in many deliberate ruins, rambling with delightful irregularity and impregnated with centuries of romantic decay. Remnants of Gothic tracery can be found in several windows, while tall arches give the structure a brooding appearance. On the west side, a broken turret looks as though it may once have been intended as a belfry, while nearby a moss-covered stone cross lies broken on the ground. Over two centuries on, Bernard's erstwhile eyecatcher, now screened from view by dense undergrowth, is far more ruinous than he could ever have imagined.

CURRY RIVEL

On Troy Hill, overlooking the Somerset Levels, stands the **Burton Pynsent Monument** (ST376252), also known as the Pynsent Steeple or the Cider Monument, looking like a finely-turned Tuscan chess-piece gleaming in the sun. A landmark for miles around, its base alone stands some nine metres high, while the tower rises to about 42 metres. No less than £2,000 was lavished on this monument to commemorate Sir William Pynsent – a man who is forgotten today and was little better known in his own time. The man responsible for building the monument, however, was one of the eighteenth century's most famous politicians.

Pynsent's only son died in 1754. Ten years later he decided to bequeath his estate to his political hero, William Pitt the Elder. Pitt's opposition to the tax on cider (during which he coined the phrase 'an Englishman's home is his castle') had endeared him to the people of Somerset. None, however, showed their gratitude in such a fulsome way as Sir William Pynsent, who expressed the wish in his will that Pitt 'will like my Burton estate … well enough to make it his country seat'.

A year later, Pynsent died, and Pitt travelled down to Somerset, writing to his wife that 'I propose to pass the rest of my days [there] if I find the place tolerable'. Affairs of state intervened, however: the following year he became prime minister and was elevated to the peerage as the Earl of Chatham. He was, nevertheless, keen to develop the estate and in September 1765 engaged 'Capability' Brown, whom he had met at Stowe, to draw up plans for landscaping the park and building a monument to his benefactor. Brown's design for the monument, which recalled Lord Cobham's Column at Stowe, which he had designed over 15 years earlier, was sent to Pitt a few months later with an accompanying note:

> I have sent by your steward a design for the Pillar which I hope will merit your approbation; if there are any parts which you disapprove of we can very easily correct them when I shall have the Honor of seeing you. The figure I have put on the pedistal is that of Gratitude, conveying to Posterity the name of Pinsent; which indeed he himself has distinguished and without flattery done in the most effectual manner by making you His Heir.

The column was built 700 metres north-west of Burton Pynsent House by Philip Pear, a builder from Curry Rivel. Stone from a nearby barley field, which Pear had to dig down five metres for, was used, and the tower was faced with Portland stone. Finished in the latter half of 1767, the Pynsent Monument retained the figure of Gratitude on its cupola until the late nineteenth century when it was replaced by an urn. A plaque bears the following inscription:

> Sacred to the memory of Sir William Pynsent
> Hoc saltem sungam inani munere

Inscriptions on old monuments are often puzzling; this one, whose Latin text can be translated as 'I will at least rise from this empty burial' is particularly so. The tower itself, however, is surely one of the most elegant columns in the country, perfectly proportioned, neat and fully deserving its restoration in the early 1990s at vast expense by the John Paul Getty Trust and English Heritage.

The steps to the top are now rarely open, as they once were until one day a cow climbed to the top. There are various endings to this story and none of them

The Burton Pynsent Monument in the early twentieth century

turns out happily for the cow. The most popular says that she was persuaded back down, but got a taste for climbing, and on her third attempt fell off. But local poet and cider-maker James Crowden says there was only one visit. Finding it impossible to turn her round, the farmer had the unfortunate animal slaughtered at the top and lowered down in pieces.

DUNSTER

High on its Tor above the Bristol Channel, **Dunster Castle** (SS991434) offers not only an impressive sight but also a thousand years of history. Despite being besieged twice during the Civil War, the absence of any buildings from before the thirteenth century is due to demolition rather than conflict. From 1376 to 1976, when the National Trust took over, Dunster was the property of the Luttrells. The intervening centuries saw the gradual development of the castle, with numerous masons and craftsmen being engaged to carry out the wishes of successive generations of Luttrells. One of the few whose name has come down to us was Anthony Salvin, the celebrated Victorian architect who specialised in rebuilding castles in the medieval style. He rebuilt the North Front around 1870, creating a richly textured interior with fine plasterwork, carving and panelling.

When William De Mohun established a castle at Dunster in the eleventh century, the sea lapped against its lower defences at high tide. Over the centuries

The Gazebo at Dunster Castle

the sea retreated and, by the time Samuel and Nathaniel Buck produced an engraving of the castle in 1733, what was once the foreshore had become pastureland. The engraving also shows an octagonal, brick-built **Gazebo** with a mullioned window from the fifteenth-century keep, demolished to make way for a bowling green. In 1741 it was recorded that the gazebo had 'a stove grate and huffer, fire shovel, tongs and poker, and four pieces of hunting chace', together with 'a mahogany octagonal table and eight leather-bottomed chairs with walnutt frames'. This indicates that the gazebo was intended as a place for the Luttrells to hold dinner parties, with the food cooked on the premises. A lead pipe head bears the Luttrell arms and the date 1727, which puts it in the time of Alexander Luttrell, but as he was only 22 at the time we cannot be sure of his influence on the project. In the late twentieth century an iron weathervane depicting a fox was added to the flat roof.

Absent from the 1733 engraving but visible on a watercolour from 1752 is a pagoda-roofed hut standing on level ground between the Tor and the River Avill. It is long gone, however, and there is no record of what it may have been used for.

It was Alexander's son-in-law, Henry Fownes Luttrell (1723-80), who made the biggest impact on the landscape around Dunster. In the 1760s and 1770s he created a deer park in the lower grounds, while on Conygar Hill to the north of the village he planted trees and built two follies. The first of these, the **Sham**

Ruin, was built on the western escarpment of the hill and is not obvious to the casual observer. It is a confection of towers and walls of the kind often built by

eighteenth-century parvenus who wished to create the impression that they had been around for a very long time. Quite why Henry was so keen to add an air of faux antiquity to the estate, when his family had lived in a medieval castle for four centuries, is unclear. The Sham Ruin is about 12 metres long, with a 90-degree turn at the east end where there is a short arch. The central part, through

Richard Phelps' drawing of the Sham Ruin

which a public footpath runs, consists of a plain thin arch with round roofless turrets on either side. The western turret is about three metres high; the eastern turret is a metre taller and has a broken upper window. There is no evidence of any holes where beams would have been inserted to create an upper storey for observation purposes, adding to the impression that this was a pure sham. However, illustrations from the period indicate that it would have been a prime spot for looking along the coast. A drawing by Richard Phelps, who may have designed the Sham Ruin, shows it much more intact than it is today and with a flag flying from one of the turrets.

Much better known, due to its prominence, is the **Conygar Hill Tower,** completed in 1775 and probably also by Richard Phelps. It cost Henry Luttrell

£76 11s 0½d for materials and labour, with £4 2s 6d spent on scrumpy for the workmen and £2 5s on an entertainment to celebrate its completion. Standing about 18 metres high, it is a round red-rubble sandstone tower tapering slightly towards a crenellated top and pierced in a regular pattern by four open entrances at ground level and four pointed windows on the

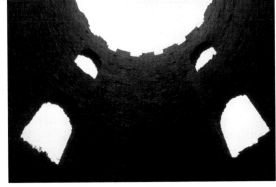

Conygar Hill Tower

two levels above. There is no evidence that it ever had floors or a roof and was probably intended solely as an eyecatcher from the castle half a mile away.

EAST HARPTREE

Harptree Court (ST568560) is a fine Regency residence built shortly after 1800 for the Waldegraves when they extended their grounds out from the village of East Harptree. It is not known whether Charles Harcourt Masters, who designed Sydney Gardens in Bath (qv), built the house, although the grounds have been attributed to him. He converted 16 fields into a 30-acre park and created two small lakes with a stream running between them. Near the stream is a **Grotto** made of local stone and tufa. It consists of a subterranean passage about 1.3 metres high, divided into two sections, each about 20 metres long, and linked by a circular court, luxuriant with ferns.

Near the upper lake is a **Rotunda**, in a very austere style with five columns supporting a dome with a ball finial at the top, probably built as an eyecatcher from the house. A little way away an icehouse can also be found hidden deep in the woods.

The Grotto and Rotunda
in the grounds of
Harptree Court

EASTON-IN-GORDANO

After years of neglect, the **Gazebo** in the grounds of **Ham Green Hospital** (ST533758), near Pill, on the south bank of the River Avon, has finally received some attention. In 1999, after featuring on Save Britain's Heritage's list of buildings at risk, the NHS announced that it would fund its restoration. The site was surveyed by archaeologist James Russell not only to ensure that the restoration of the gazebo was historically accurate but also to discover more about the gardens that once surrounded it.

The hexagonal gazebo occupies the tip of a low terrace. Although it has been a hollow, roofless shell for many years, it still retains some Gothick features such as ogee heads to the windows and crenellation on the parapet. Built of brick with freestone dressings on a coursed rubble base, it dates from around 1760, and may have been built by James Bridges. It originally had an ogee-profiled dome terminating in a ball finial.

By the end of the eighteenth century Ham Green House was occupied by Richard Bright, a wealthy Bristol merchant with scientific and cultural interests. Around 1799 he built a small rectangular annexe on the south-west side of the gazebo where he carried out experiments on gases and minerals. A watercolour by Bright's wife shows the annexe with small statues in canopied niches around the walls. The annexe was demolished around 1841, and, apart from the roofline visible above the door of the gazebo, few traces of it were found during the archaeological survey. It is a great shame that the annexe has gone because it is likely that it was here that Sir Humphrey Davy joined Bright in his experiments. The two men might also have inspired Bright's son, also called Richard, to follow a scientific career which culminated in his discovery of chronic nephritis, the kidney disease which is more commonly known as Bright's Disease.

The Gazebo at Ham Green

At the bottom of the cliff below the gazebo can be found the **Adam & Eve Towers**. Averaging just over three metres high, this curious structure consists mainly of a semi-circular whitewashed curtain wall – once pierced by an arch which is now blocked up – curving towards two low towers close to the river. Once used as a landing stage for Ham Green House, it has given rise to a variety of legends. According to one, slaves were landed here in the eighteenth century and taken by an underground passage to Ham Green House. According to another, the turrets at either end were built by an outraged father in order to imprison his daughter and her lover. Separated by just ten metres, they would have been able to hear each other's plaintive sighs but not to see each other. This legend may have derived from the figures of Adam and Eve which stand on either side of the arch. GS Hart in his book on Ham Green says that these caryatid-like ornaments may be pre-Renaissance in origin and have once decorated a mantelpiece in an earlier Ham Green House.

Today, with a flashing light on a pole fixed to the eastern tower, the Adam & Eve Towers are still a navigational aid for shipping. They also form the logo of the Port of Bristol Authority Social Club, which stands on the opposite bank of the river in Shirehampton. It was from this spot in 1789 that SH Grimm, a local artist, drew 'Mr Bright's Pleasure Ground', complete with Gazebo, Towers, and a ship docked at low tide.

ELWORTHY

While the Quantocks bristle with all sorts of follies, especially towers, the Brendons lack such ornamentation, possibly because of the bleaker nature of the countryside and the lack of large estates. The **Willett Tower** (ST095335) is an exception, and comes in the shape of a sham church tower which Greenwood, in his book on Somersetshire (1822), described as 'a fine object to the country for many miles around'. Like many buildings with no apparent function, the local population were not slow in coming up with reasons for its construction. One legend has it that it saw action in the Civil War, another that it was built for a lady living in Willett House who spent much of her time admiring the view from a 'bower' at the top. Pevsner, who claims it was built by a Mr Belmerton in 1820, describes it as 'a copy of a ruined Somerset Church Tower [with] an attached piece of the ruined church … specially erected to reinforce the effect'.

The Willett Tower

Collinson, however, in his History and Antiquities of the County of Somerset (1791), recorded that the tower had been 'erected a few years since, at the expence of the local gentry'. It seems to have been built around 1774, being paid for by a public subscription of £130, £80 of which came from James Bernard, who also built follies in the grounds of Crowcombe Manor. This relatively low figure suggests that the tower never had an interior, but was used simply as a beacon.

It stands around 15 metres high. Some of its lower parts have crumbled away and thick buttresses suggest that there may once have been a nave extending from the tower. A wing halfway along the south side of the tower juts out with one window, begging the question of whether the wall originally extended further. There is evidence of recent remedial work, with stones and slates having been cemented into place, and there is also a collapsed wall on the north side, suggesting some symmetry. At one time, a wooden staircase led up to the battlemented top, but this has long since disappeared.

FARLEIGH HUNGERFORD

The estate around **Farleigh House** (ST798570) has a history stretching back to the fourteenth century when Sir Thomas Hungerford, speaker of the House of Commons, built the now ruinous Farleigh Castle. Eventually the Hungerfords sold the estate, most of which came into the possession of Trowbridge clothier Joseph Houlton in the eighteenth century. His son, Joseph Houlton Junior, turned an old gabled farmhouse into a gentleman's residence which he called Farleigh House (also confusingly known as Farleigh Castle at one time) about a mile to the south-west of the old castle. The Farleigh estate was developed during this period, with Houlton creating a 120-acre deer park. It was not until the time of Colonel John Houlton, however, that it started to acquire significant embellishments. After inheriting the estate in 1806, he spent some £40,000 on hothouses, conservatories, stables and no less than six lodges. Houlton favoured the Gothic Revival style, which he used to remodel the façade of the house, as well as building sham fortifications such as a 15-metre-high hexagonal tower.

The **Grotto**, built in 1806 of random rubble and ashlar stone from Doulting, is now a mossy, overgrown pile. In better shape is the neighbouring screen wall, which extends some 170 metres to the west of the house. There is also some ornamental walling near the house, including a large niche-cum-summerhouse, with a coat-of-arms in the centre of the façade. However, if anything in the grounds is a folly it is the Curtain Wall which forms the entrance to the house and is embellished with crenellations, arrowslits and three-metre-high turrets. A small pointed door has been inserted into the wall, somewhat redundantly as it leads nowhere in particular and looks out over a ha-ha and the field beyond. At the other end of the wall is a **Sham Chapel**, which has been extended so that on the other side it looks like a normal cottage. However, on the side facing Farleigh House it is a riot of pinnacles and crenellations, while the west side has a blind window with some fine tracery.

The Sham Chapel at Farleigh Hungerford

Originally part of the same estate, but sold off many years ago, is **Bath Lodge** (ST787563), the largest of the six lodges built by Houlton. Situated on the busy A36, it was built between

1806 and 1813 in the style of a small medieval castle, with circular towers and crenellated parapets. In the main body of the lodge is a mullioned and transomed window with diamond-leaded panes, while arrowslit and cruciform windows light the way up the towers. It is flanked by embattled walls with circular towers halfway along, and low square towers at the corners. In the late twentieth century the lodge was extended in a sympathetic way in order to accommodate a hotel.

Bath Lodge

GOATHURST

The awful shade, the solemn stilness of the scene, broken by nothing but the fall of distant waters, have altogether a great effect, and impress upon the mind a melancholy scarcely effaced by the cheerful view of a rich vale, with the water winding through it, which is seen on crossing the park towards the house. This seat has received rich gifts from nature, and very pleasing ones from art ... The whole scene is really elegant; every part is riant, and bears the stamp of pleasure.

Such were Arthur Young's impressions of **Halswell House** (ST254337) in 1768. In the same year Sir Charles Kemeys-Tynte added no less than four follies to the estate. Halswell was favoured by natural springs as well as fine soil and views northwards to the Bristol Channel. The first house on the site was built by the Halswell family in 1536. In the mid-seventeenth century, Jane Halswell, the last of the line, married John Tynte of Chelvey. Their son, Halswell Tynte, who was created a baronet in 1674, rebuilt the north range of the house in 1689, possibly using William Taylor as his surveyor. It is likely that Sir Halswell or his son John, who died in 1710, also created a formal garden with a substantial parterre and terraces, as well as two brick and stone pavilions.

By 1740, when Sir Charles came into the baronetcy, the fashion in gardens had changed to the more natural English style, and over the next 44 years he transformed the estate to reflect contemporary taste. One of the first buildings to adorn the gardens was a curious **Stepped Pyramid** near the house, surmounted by the family emblem – a griffin supporting a shield – and covering a spring running into a tank. At one time, according to Barbara Jones, there was an inscription on the pyramid – 'this Edifice was created in Honour of a pure nymph' – which may have been provided by Alexander Pope.

Richard Escott, who has left an invaluable account of the estate's development, was appointed its steward by Kemeys-Tynte in 1753. The estate's transformation from the formal to the informal style had already started by the time he arrived, and coincided with the conversion of a canal on the east side of the house to a serpentine lake. At the north end of the lake a **Rockwork Screen**, which formed part of a dam, was built. This consists of a façade with a blind arch, about three metres high, with massive stones curving round the top, flanked by two niches. It is probable that water once trickled down from the lake through the screen and into a large round pond which has since disappeared.

A short distance away on a mound stands **Mrs Busby's Temple**, named after Lady Kemeys-Tynte's sister. Possibly built by John de Wilstar, the surveyor responsible for the 1756 estate map, it is a standard Doric rotunda, with a decorated frieze around the entablature. It is currently being restored. An icehouse was built below the rotunda in 1767.

High on a hill to the south, overlooking the park, stands **Robin Hood's Hut**, sometimes known as Robin Hood's Temple. Admiration for the hero of Sherwood Forest in the eighteenth century sometimes led to the creation of follies suggesting a wider geographical range than even Hollywood dared. Another of Kemeys-Tynte's landscaping friends, John Aislabie, built his own temple to Robin Hood, now gone, at Studley Royal in Yorkshire, while Kemeys-Tynte's agent's house was called Sherwood. The coup of surprise on stumbling across Robin Hood's Hut was engineered by Kemeys-Tynte. Visitors followed a serpentine drive up through the woods till they came upon a rustic door covered in bark, with a thatched roof above, a fitting abode for a man of the greenwood. This was the back of the building. The front was in an airy, Strawberry Hill Gothick style, and commanded extensive views. It was probably designed by Henry Keene, Surveyor of the Fabric of Westminster Abbey, and almost certainly owes a debt to Batty Langley's pattern books. Keene's original design had an array of ornate pinnacles, turrets and crenellations, although he eventually settled for a simpler design. Two splendid ogee windows flank an 'umbrellero' or short open verandah, with three ogee

Robin Hood's Hut before and after restoration

arches projecting as a terrace and forming part of an octagon, with a simple neo-classical frieze above. Kemeys-Tynte's specifications for the building were very specific. In 1767, for example, he gave instructions that 'the first room, which I call the hermit's room, must have an earthen floor, the kitchen on the left, a brick, and the little room for china, must be board'd'.

After years of dereliction and vandalism, in 1999 the building was rebuilt by the Landmark Trust and painted yellow, making it visible for miles around. The views from the Hut, which can now be rented out as a holiday cottage, are superb, and, when the estate was originally laid out, would have taken in most if not all of the other follies. Today, however, most of the follies are obscured by trees. One that can still be seen is the Dovecote, built of cob, with a beautifully curved, bell-shaped slate roof topped by a small belfry. Built into the back of the long range of the riding school, it used to stand close to a neatly laid out garden and covers one of the many springs of Halswell.

Now cut off from the rest of the estate, Mill Wood was once an almost sacred grove of delights. At the top of a series of ponds, near a bridge overhung with trees, was the **Druid's Temple**. Built in 1756, it was based on a design that formed the frontispiece to Thomas Wright's Book of Arbours, which had been published the previous year. Both Kemeys-Tynte and his architect, Thomas Prowse of Axbridge, subscribed to Wright's book, which was a collection of architectural drawings aimed at landowners wishing to hark back to the days of the ancient Britons in their landscape gardens. The temple was octagonal and built of wood, with tree trunks for columns and a pyramidal thatched roof. There was a door at the back, but it is not clear whether this opened into a room or directly outside. Arthur Young described the view of the temple as 'gloomy and confined; the water winds silently along, except for a little gushing fall, which hurts not the emotions raised by so sequestered a scene'. Nothing remains of this building, and considering the fragile nature of its construction and the general neglect of the estate, it is remarkable that it survived until the 1950s.

Close to the site of the Druid's Temple are the remains of a **Grotto**, consisting of three rustic stone niches overhung with vegetation. One niche has a series of stone shelves, while another used to contain a well-head flanked by a tablet inscribed with the following lines:

> When Israel's wandering sons the desert trod,
> The melting rock obey'd the prophet's rod,
> Forth gushed the stream; the tribes their thirst allay'd,
> Forgetful of their God, they rose, and play'd.
> Ye happy swains, for whom these waters flow,
> O may your hearts with grateful ardours glow;
> Lo! Here a fountain streams, at his command,
> Not o'er a barren but fruitful land;
> Where nature's choicest gifts the vallies fill,
> And smiling plenty gladdens every hill.

A little way down the hill one of the dams is disguised as a **Bridge**, built of Bath Stone in 1755. It is considerably decayed and large pieces of masonry have fallen off, but it is still an impressive sight. It consists of a large niche with alternate smooth and vermiculated stone. To the right, the niche is buttressed by a wall falling away to a low balustrade. On the left side the buttress is broken, but on the right it is reasonably intact with massive rude stones on the top. On a plinth at the end of the balustrade a female half-figure garlanded with shells rises from carved foliage and flowers. The sculpture at the other end of the balustrade has disappeared.

The design is something of an oddity, not conforming to any of the classical models of garden buildings. It may have been inspired by Wright's drawings for a 'River Head' and a 'Break Water', but there is also a strong possibility that Kemeys-Tynte was more than a mere copyist. In a portrait attributed to Hogarth, he is depicted with the bridge under construction in the background, and a volume entitled Garden Plans and a set of drawing instruments on the table in front of him, suggesting he designed the bridge himself. Further down the valley between the fourth and the fifth ponds stands a six-metre-tall rubble-stone pillar, all that remains of a rustic stone-arched structure through which the water flowed past a statue of Neptune.

The last of the buildings to be constructed on this side of the estate was the **Temple of Harmony**, designed by Thomas Prowse in 1764 in memory of Peregrine Palmer, MP for the University of Oxford, who had died two years previously and was a friend of Kemeys-Tynte and Prowse. Based on the Temple of Fortuna Virilis in the Forum Boarium in Rome, it is a neat Ionic tetrastyle temple, with an additional column on each side, and topped by a simple pediment. The aedicule or neo-classical niche in the inside end wall was probably taken from a design by Robert Adam, with Palmyra columns, but with a sarcophagus panel instead of the

The Temple of Harmony before and after restoration

decorative one proposed by Adam. The original plasterwork was by Thomas Stocking of Bristol.

To commemorate Prowse's own death in 1767, a marble statue of Terpsichore was made by John Walsh, who was paid the sum of £44 in 1768, and then, for some reason, another £85 four years later. Terpsichore was the Muse of Song and Dance in Roman mythology, but, as Prowse was an architect, Walsh shows her not only holding a zither in her left hand but also a pair of compasses in her right, symbolising the harmonious nature of architecture and mathematics as well as music. The statue at Halswell today is a copy by Philip Thomason from Cudworth near Ilminster, who has revived the production of Coade stone; the original is in the County Museum at Taunton.

If the follies around Mill Wood seem isolated from the house and the rest of the estate, the brick-built **Temple of Pan** is even more remote. Situated at Patcombe Farm, away to the south-west, it was the bailiff's house and got its name from a statue of Pan which once stood nearby. When the estate was broken up in 1950, the statue went to Castle Hill in North Devon, but, after a long period of dereliction, the 'temple' was restored as a dwelling house in 1997. While its design may not stick faithfully to classical models, its Doric bay colonnade and oriel window high in the façade have a certain charm. It was built in 1771 by John Johnson the Elder, who also built the riding school on the estate, and was County Surveyor of Essex between 1782 and 1812. He exhibited a drawing of the Temple at the Society of Artists in 1778.

The figure of Terpsichore in the Temple of Harmony and the Temple of Pan at Patcombe

In 1994, after decades of neglect, the Halswell Park Trust was created to oversee the restoration of the Temple of Harmony and Robin Hood's Hut. The Somerset Buildings Preservation Trust funded the restoration of the Temple of Harmony while the Landmark Trust rebuilt Robin Hood's Hut. The Trust also has plans to recreate a Monument to Sir Charles's favourite horse, a sarcophagus on a plinth surmounted by an urn which once stood between the house and Mill Wood. Constructed in 1765, and based on Thomas Wright's monument to the fourth Duke of Beaufort at Stoke Park in Bristol, it was demolished in 1950.

HENSTRIDGE

Inwood House (ST712202), a large, irregular two-storey stone building with gabled attics, was built in 1881 by the Welsh industrialist Thomas Merthyr Guest on the site of an earlier house. The grounds were relandscaped but some earlier features were retained. These included a **Water Tower**, which stands 20 metres

south of the stable block. Built of local grey-coursed rubble stone and brick, it is circular and has a crenellated parapet hiding a flat roof. It is strengthened with iron straps above the string courses and was further strengthened by four large curving buttresses in the early twentieth century. Standing over twelve metres high and consisting of four storeys, its walls are pierced haphazardly by arched windows and decorated with a series of wrought-iron shields at various points.

A short distance away and backing onto the stables stands the Temple of Laocoon, a small Doric temple built of Portland stone and brick, with a broken segmental pediment. Inside on a plinth is a bronze copy of the famous sculpture of Laocoon in the Vatican. The story of Laocoon is one of defiance that ended violently. When the Greeks presented the Trojan Horse to the citizens of Troy, Laocoon warned them against accepting it – the origin of the phrase, 'beware of Greeks bearing gifts'. The gods responded by sending snakes from the sea to strangle and poison him along with his sons, who are curiously sculpted in miniature alongside the life-size muscular figure of Laocoon struggling in agony. The Trojans ignored Laocoon's advice, brought the Horse into the city, and the rest is history. The Inwood Laocoon is one of several in this country, but is believed to be the only one in the open air.

While the Temple of Laocoon follows classical orders, the **Oriental**

The Water Tower, Oriental Summerhouse and Temple of Laocoon in the grounds of Inwood House at Henstridge

Summerhouse, which Thomas Guest is believed to have imported from Italy, is a piece of pure whimsy. A gold-painted cast-iron ball finial terminates a copper onion dome which slopes down to a wide canopy edged with elaborate metalwork. At the head of each wrought-iron supporting pier is a gargoyle in the form of a golden dragon's head. Golden bells supported by curved wrought iron supports hang above the dragons' heads. Sheltering under the canopy is a large urn decorated with elephants' heads, dogs and puppies, and a dragon spout at the front.

HESTERCOMBE

For many years the main delight of **Hestercombe** (ST243288) was the garden designed by Gertrude Jekyll and Sir Edwin Lutyens, with its attractive pergolas, rills, paving and planting. Few visitors ventured behind the house to wander in the combe, a lost world of overgrown vegetation, with the odd ruined folly and paths that led nowhere. Some follies and other features had completely disappeared or were only traceable from their foundation stones. Then around 1990 things began to stir when Philip White, who was working at Hestercombe for the Somerset Wildlife Trust, remortgaged his house in order to fund one of the most important restorations of a landscape garden that Somerset has ever seen. The attention to detail in recreating the original designs of Coplestone Warre Bampfylde has been painstaking, and has paid off in the form of a small Eden just a few miles from Taunton.

Bampfylde was a book illustrator and artist who was a close friend of two influential garden designers, Henry Hoare of Stourhead and Sir Charles Kemeys-Tynte of Halswell (qv). Hestercombe had been in the possession of the Warre family since 1391 but it was not until 1750, when Bampfylde inherited the 55-acre estate, that anything truly memorable was created there. The only major feature that predated him was the **Pear Pond**, so-called because of its shape, which was there by 1698. Bampfylde built a carriage drive around the pond and extended it up the combe past a series of picturesque and charming landscape features. Then, in 1761, along a path high on the eastern side of the combe, he built the first in a series of follies. A viewpoint, known as **Capriccio View**, and approached down a side path, was constructed on the other side of the valley, to give visitors a foretaste of the delights that awaited them once they had toiled up the slopes on the far side. The first three follies to be built – a Mausoleum, a Witch House and a Gothic Alcove – were all visible from Capriccio View.

The **Mausoleum**, situated on a slight rise overlooking Pear Pond, is unusual both in shape and appearance. Painted dark pink, with a heavy vermiculated stone arch for an entrance, it has two piers supporting urns at either end of the façade. Above this the façade sweeps up to a truncated obelisk on a rusticated base, about six metres high. Inside is a simple chamber, curved at the back. It is unlikely that

The Mausoleum from Capriccio View

Bampfylde intended to place a tomb in the mausoleum; it was almost certainly intended solely to remind visitors of the mausoleums of antiquity, as a memento mori in the Arcadian landscape. An inscription on a stone set into the façade includes a quatrain from an early version of Pope's Windsor Forest:

> Happy the man who to the shades retires
> Whom Nature charms, and whom the Muse inspires
> Blest whom the Sweets of home-felt Quiet please
> But far more blest, who Study joins with Ease.

The Mausoleum was the only folly to survive, albeit in a very parlous state, the dereliction which overtook Hestercombe in the nineteenth and twentieth centuries. It is hard to believe, looking at it today, that, when it was listed in 1984, it was described as being in poor condition.

The **Witch House**, on top of a steep slope above the mausoleum, and built of wood, tree roots and thatch, disappeared completely. The present structure, based on the original design, dates from 1998. On either side of the opening are two 'swags' of wood like drapes which follow the curved form of branches.

The Witch House: Tasteful Enchantment

The left swag has a sculpted snake slithering up it. Inside, on the back wall, are wooden plaques painted with whimsically talismanic images: a cat, an owl, a snake and a witch on a broomstick. The chamber is furnished with three round seats fashioned from the trunks of trees and two benches. Twigs and roots curl their way up short tree trunks and bosses of wood finish off the design. Despite its

Paradise Restored: the Gothic Alcove, Friendship Urn and Temple Arbour at Hestercombe, originally built by Coplestone Warre Bampfylde in the eighteenth century and now recreated on their original sites

occult trappings, Bampfylde's aim in building the folly was no more sinister than to cast a spell of enchantment over his visitors. As the Vicar of Blagdon (who would certainly have had no truck with the occult) wrote:

> O'er Bampfylde's woods by various nature graced
> A witch presides, but then that witch was Taste.

A couple of hundred metres beyond the Witch House is the **Temple Arbour**, a tetrastyle Doric temple with a plain, open interior and a dado rail running along the wall at waist height. Originally built around 1775, and now rebuilt to the original design, it stands on a slight rise looking across to the Witch House and down the valley to the Friendship Urn. The influence of Hoare, who developed the art of making follies visible from each other, thereby creating a constantly changing series of goals to move towards, can be seen clearly in the disposition of Bampfylde's follies at this point.

The eastern path flattens out as it progresses up the combe, giving the visitor glimpses of the valley below and, on the far side, an impressive **Cascade**, built in 1762 and influenced by a cascade at the Leasowes in Worcestershire created by William Shenstone. So impressive was Shenstone's cascade that Henry Temple, 2nd Viscount Palmerston, was moved to declare it 'one of the best things of the kind I have seen in the territory of a private person'. Long choked by vegetation, restoration work has seen Bampfylde's cascade restored to its original splendour; seen after heavy rain, it is indeed a prodigious spectacle.

The most far-flung of the follies, at the edge of the estate, was the **Gothic Alcove**, a small crenellated gothic building. The original, dating from 1761, disappeared years ago, but it has now been rebuilt and visitors can once again sit and enjoy the prospect southwards over the Vale of Taunton Deane, surrounded by what to all intents and purposes appears a relic from the middle ages.

In 1786, Bampfylde added the final touch to his Arcadian landscape – a **Friendship Urn** in honour of Hoare and Kemeys Tynte with an inscription containing a quotation from Horace's Satires which can be translated as:

> Earth has not borne such shining spirits as these
> Nor any with whom I have closer bonds.

In 1963, the urn, which was in very poor state of repair, with several pieces missing, was moved to the orangery. Its replacement, based on the original, was made by Mel N Morris Jones of Dulverton for the Western Provident Association and donated to the gardens in 1997 to mark their reopening.

The programme of restoration at Hestercombe which will lead to more follies being rebuilt. In time, it is hoped that an Octagonal Summerhouse, a Chinese Seat and a Rustic Seat, whose sites have been established by archaeological surveys, will reappear at the points where they were allowed to crumble to dust. Bampfylde's Paradise is slowly, but methodically, being regained.

Detail from the Friendship Urn

HUNSTRETE

The fate of **Hunstrete House** (ST647622) is a salutary tale of how swiftly dreams of glory can crumble to nothing. Once one of the largest houses in Somerset, with a 17-bay front, nothing of it now remains except a row of five arches which formed one of the walls of the drawing room. In the 1770s, Sir Francis Popham decided to build a Bath stone mansion near the site of the old manor house of the abbots of Glastonbury. The estate was also remodelled and six lakes created. Sir Francis died in 1779, soon after work had started, but his widow carried on with his plans until her death in 1797. Despite at least £30,000 having been spent on it, the house was still incomplete, and Sir Francis's heir, General Leyborne Popham, decided to remain on his estate at Littlecote on the Wiltshire/Berkshire border rather than move to Somerset. For over 30 years Hunstrete House lay empty and vulnerable to the predations of the elements; by 1831 it had deteriorated to such an extent that General Popham ordered its demolition. Some of the landscaping planned by Sir Francis – including an icehouse set into the hillside – can still be seen today, although much of the estate is now covered by a lake used by anglers.

The arches at Hunstrete

The arches, stripped of their rendering, stand as a solitary reminder of a once great house that sadly never became a home. Its main doorway was incorporated into the nearby Hunstrete House Hotel, but most of the masonry was dispersed elsewhere, some of it to Prior Park in Bath to replace masonry destroyed after a disastrous fire in 1836.

ILTON

Few shell houses are as spellbinding as **Jordan's** (ST337162). The eighteenth-century house to which the shell house belonged has now gone, but there remains this little gem, built in 1828 by William Speke. He was one of several men called William in a family best known for John Hanning Speke, who discovered the source of the Nile in 1862. The Shell House's relatively recent iron gate is a reminder of Speke's African adventures, for the word NILE and the family's coat of arms with a crocodile and hippopotamus have been wrought into the design. The materials used to decorate the shell house are less exotic; except for the coral, they all come from Somerset.

Once through the gate, the interior opens up like an Aladdin's cave of wonders, richly decorated and coloured. The ceiling of the central chamber is covered with shells in the shape of a star, while the table in the centre of the room has conches and other shells arranged on it and stuck onto its base. The walls are encrusted with ammonites, sea-urchins and shells set in floral patterns, and the back wall has a frieze running along its length. Below this is a mirror reflecting three lozenge-shaped stained-glass windows at the front, each with a Virgin and Child motif, which cast coloured light over the shells.

A wicker-topped seat curves round the back wall. Sheep's knucklebones form much of the floor, and the door-frame has coral and long shells hanging down in keeping with the style of the building.

Jordan's Shell House: like a jewel box hidden in a hedgerow

Out of place is the portico, which is starting to separate from the wall, and has a curved roof and columns with capitals of grapes and leaves. The two side chambers contrast with the central chamber by being predominantly white with black and white shell decoration, most notably black mussel shells set into the window frames. The chambers both have basins which once spurted water when operated by the servants, but they are now dry. Wire grilles protect the window glass, but the shutters are half open, suggesting that the canaries which once occupied the nesting holes, decorated with shells to look like the branches of a tree, have long since flown. The Shell House, which is thatched and has a small cupola with a weathervane in the shape of fish, is a magical place, and its location, near a pond and on the edge of the woods, only adds to its feeling of romantic seclusion.

KILMERSDON

Rivalry and revenge surround the **Ammerdown Column** (ST718522), a striking shaft of stone in the Georgian style erected near Kilmersdon on a slight rise to the east of Ammerdown House. Now a residential conference centre, the house was built for Thomas Samuel Jolliffe by James Wyatt in 1788. In the mid-nineteenth century, Jolliffe's son, Colonel John Twyford Jolliffe, engaged Joseph Jopling to build a 48-metre-high column to commemorate his father. Over 30 years earlier, Jopling had written an architectural treatise entitled The Septenary System of Drawing Curves, so it is not surprising that the Ammerdown Column was designed with a graceful curvature at the bottom of the shaft and curlicues of stone like the strokes of a pen on the plinth-cum-terrace at the base. The

Towering ambitions: the Ammerdown Column early last century with its lighthouse-like lantern; the Ammerdown Column today; Turner's Tower

corners of the terrace were embellished by four Coade-stone statues but these were later moved to the garden near the house. Colonel Jolliffe did not live to see the completion of the column in June 1855, for he died in 1854 after a long illness caused by a fall from a horse.

The column rests on a small square room with oval windows in its chamfered sides. On the west, north and east sides are faded inscriptions in English, Latin and French, praising Thomas Jolliffe's achievement in reclaiming the surrounding heath for grazing and cultivation. The column tapers smoothly before straightening out for 30 metres or so and then reaching some decorative mouldings. Immediately above these the tower bulges out to support a a plinth which projects about a metre from the shaft of the column. The final embellishment was a glass lantern containing the Jolliffe crest in the form of a crown, with a pinnacle on top. When the sun reflected from the lantern, it could be seen from miles away, and not surprisingly it came to be known as the Ammerdown Lighthouse. The lantern survived until the 1970s, when, after the pinnacle toppled over and the windows were blown in, it was declared unsafe and dismantled.

One man who would have enjoyed the lantern's fate was John Turner, a quarry owner from the neighbouring village of Faulkland. After losing a lawsuit against Lord Hylton, who had inherited the Ammerdown Estate through the descendants of Thomas Jolliffe's elder brother, Turner decided to wreak his revenge by outdoing the Ammerdown Column. He knew that Lord Hylton was a shy and retiring man, and would be dismayed at the prospect of having his estate overlooked, especially by him, and so he bought the highest available plot of land near Ammerdown and proceeded to build **Turner's Tower**.

At 54 metres, Turner's Tower was six metres higher than the Ammerdown Column. It was a square, thin structure in a vaguely Italianate style, which narrowed towards the top in stages, each with its own balcony. Built mainly of local stone, the last six metres were of timber, with a chair, facing Ammerdown, at the top. To recoup his costs, Turner ran the tower as a commercial venture, and built a ballroom and tea gardens at the bottom in order to attract visitors. On the opening day, he not only provided a free banquet for the locals, but also engaged a sailor to perform a handstand on the top rung of the chair to the amazement of the crowd. A chair in the church at nearby Hemington has the inscription, 'Presented to J Turner Esq on completion of the Eiffel Tower 1890', carved on it. Was this the chair that once crowned the tower? We may never know, and cannot be any more certain whether Turner was trying to emulate the prominent Parisian landmark, or whether the donor of the chair was ridiculing his pretension.

Turner only enjoyed his view over Ammerdown for a few years, dying in 1894. By 1910 the tower had become unsafe after being struck by lightning. When the top half was demolished the stone was bought by none other than Lord Hylton in order to build a cottage on the Ammerdown estate. Since 1969, there has been virtually no evidence of the tower's existence, its remains having being demolished.

LEIGH WOODS

Many fine minerals are contained in the striking rocks of the Avon Gorge, including the so-called 'Bristol diamonds', a type of quartz, but none of them found their way into the rock garden created at the house above the gorge known as **Rayne Thatch** (ST558731). Originally known as the Bungalow, despite having two floors, it was built in 1907 as an estate office for Bracken Hill, the seat of the tobacco entrepreneur Captain Melville Wills on the other side of North Road. By building in the chalet style, Wills may have wished it to fit in with the wooded surroundings, creating a touch of Switzerland in Somerset, but it is more likely that he copied a cottage on his Scottish estate. To add to the Alpine atmosphere, he built a wooden verandah around the first floor, linking it to the garden by a wooden bridge, and then finished it off with a thatched roof.

Between 1908 and 1910 he employed Pulham and Son, landscape gardeners with a national reputation for artificial rock, to create a rockery covering half a hectare. The firm's technique was to gather clinker and other waste building material, and then to pour over this aggregate a mixture of Portland cement which was then moulded into individual boulders. As the cement had the colour and finish of sandstone, it was given authenticity by being arranged to suggest the natural strata of sandstone outcrops. The stones are grouped around a series of five linked pools and have been formed into alcoves, at one point reaching a height of three metres, and planted with ferns and alpines. At the west end of the largest pool, rocks jut towards each other from either side, creating a narrow opening through which a small boat can pass into a grotto-like alcove and be moored. A rocky pathway runs around the edge of the pool and takes in a picturesque view

of the house surrounded by pine, oak, ash, elm, hawthorn, birch and wild cherry trees. At one point steps lead down into the water for bathers, and from the main pool the water falls into a series of three smaller pools. When the garden was illuminated at night by hundreds of coloured lights hung in the trees, it must have made a very charming scene.

An inscription 'FH 1910' can be seen on one of the rocks between the house and the road. This may have been the mark of Fred Hitchens, the Pulham & Son foreman working here, who may also have worked at Bracken Hill after the First World War when its grounds were landscaped with both Pulhamite and natural limestone built into archways and pools. A further example of Pulhamite created for Melville Wills can be seen at Abbot's Pool at nearby Abbot's Leigh, where a dam was raised and a boathouse built on one of a chain of ornamental ponds.

LONG ASHTON

Set back from the Bristol to Nailsea road and surrounded by pleasant gardens was the **Observatory** (ST518698), otherwise known as the Dome or the Bungalow. It was built by Thomas Twigg Humpage, who is still remembered today by some local people, including Norman Yeo, who sang with him in the Long Ashton Choir:

> I was about 15 when Humpage was in his forties. He was a serious type of man. I never saw him laugh, and being an inventor he wanted to build the house his way, not with his own hands but with the help of his own factory's labour in a time when there was a depression in the engineering trade. It was temporarily abandoned when business picked up and caused a lack of labour. When I used to cycle back from Clevedon, it was easy to see because there were no trees surrounding it, and it used to stick out even more when he built the observatory on top in about 1929 or 1930.

With a squarish ground plan, the Bungalow was made almost entirely of wood, with a couple of matching bay windows with half conical roofs forming the corners of the house. The roof of the porch was pyramidal, but the rest of the

The Long Ashton Observatory, one of Somerset's most recently lost follies

roof was flat and made of asbestos and wood painted black. The whole structure had the feeling of a temporary prefab, being supported mainly on old wooden coalpit props surrounded by rocks and just one supporting concrete foundation wall running along the front of the house.

Humpage was a brilliant engineer who became a partner in the engineering firm of Humpage, Thompson & Hardy based in Jacob Street between Broadmead and St Philip's in Bristol. Around 1922, he decided to build himself a summerhouse on bare, deserted land next to what is now the B3130. Humpage had to excavate in order to level the land of a sloping field before starting to build the house. Humpage's granddaughter Mary Smallcombe remembers his interest in astronomy and his telescope, but also at being upset by a headline in a local newspaper which described the Bungalow as 'the latest monstrosity of the West', for her memories are nothing but pleasant of a building which was painted pale lemon in colour when she knew it. Her husband Leonard remembers Humpage as 'an all-rounder and a serious sort of man. He expected others to be like him, and if they weren't, he was impatient. I called him "Branchy" as a joke.'

Sheila Flowers, Humpage's great niece, went to live there as a young girl with her widowed mother who was housekeeper to a Mr Beavis, a soft drinks manufacturer who owned it after Humpage. Relatively safe from the Blitz, he made the Bungalow his home during the Second World War. She recalls that

the Beavises used to entertain wounded soldiers who were convalescing at the nearby large houses of Tyntesfield and Barrow Court. The gardens were lovely with walnut trees and everyone could play on the croquet lawn. We gave the soldiers nectarines and grapes from the greenhouse. And as for my accommodation, each night I climbed a ladder to the observatory which I had for my bedroom, but there was no electric light.

After Mr Beavis's death, his widow married a Mr Mitchell who built a curious concrete fountain at the back of the house. There is another, smaller fountain further up the hill, which, like the other, is now dry. In 1975 the house was bought by Tony Atherton, whose family had lived next door for generations. By this time much of the wood in the house was rotten, and, after having replaced the observatory in a vain attempt to halt the process of decay, in 2005 he reluctantly decided to demolish it and build a brick and stone house on the same footprint and with a circular observatory at the top.

LYMPSHAM

Lympsham, sometimes called Lymplesham, is a village with a timeless air. Its greatest architectural glory is the **Manor** (ST334542), a gothic revival fantasy, sparkling white and decorated with such a variety of buttresses, string courses, shields, pinnacles, and mullions that it almost looks like a folly in its own right. There is also a turret for composing sermons, for the Manor was built by the Reverend Joseph Adam Stephenson around 1813, shortly after he acquired the advowson. He was famous for his religious zeal and established a dynasty of cleric-squires in Lympsham at a time when it was possible to pass a living from one generation to the next. Seven years after his death in 1837, his son, Joseph Henry Stephenson, came into the benefice, remaining for 57 years until his death in 1901, during which time he was revered by many of his parishioners.

One of the pinnacles at Lympsham, their provenance unknown

There was, however, a group of dissenters, who in 1858 conducted a pampleteering campaign against Stephenson, accusing him of 'Romanism'. The recipients were so outraged at the 'monstrous absurdity' of the charge that the pamphlets were unceremoniously burned. This attack on Stephenson's character did not prevent him from erecting a joint memorial to a Methodist and an Anglican about 200 metres south of the house in 1876. It is not clear whether the memorial consisted of the whole of the

Pinnacle, or just the two plaques – now illegible – fitted on opposite sides of this highly ornate piece of masonry.

A matching pinnacle stands in the centre of the village on the corner of South Street. It is of similar design, being octagonal and five metres high, but, unlike the other one, has no openings in its niches. Rising from the bottom, the pinnacle has the following features: a trefoil frieze, pointed niches, a drip mould, smaller trefoils about 15 centimetres in diameter, narrower niches, little projections, a tapering spire and a finial in the shape of a cross, with one broken segment. It bears three plaques: the first has the inscription, 'Love one another', the second, 'Fear God', while the third, although nearly illegible, seems to have read, 'Honour the King', completing the quotation from the First Epistle of Peter. The two pinnacles most likely were gateposts at an entrance to the manor, though they may also have formed part of a church.

MARSTON BIGOT

Here hangs the villa in majestick show
And high in beauty fronts the meads below
And seated thus, looks to the distant eye
Like some enchanted palace in the sky
From Marston House by Samuel Bowden, 1733

Marston House (ST757453) is one of several great Somerset houses to have known changing fortunes, and was once almost ready for the demolition hammer. Its heyday was in the eighteenth century, and over the centuries it has benefited from a series of enthusiastic, if sometimes penniless, owners, the first of whom was Richard Boyle, created Earl of Cork in 1641. After it passed to his youngest son, the 1st Earl of Orrery, it entered a period of decline which ended when the 4th Earl of Cork and Orrery inherited. The house was remodelled by John Boyle, the 5th Earl, who also redesigned the estate with the help of James Scott and Stephen Switzer. Switzer, who arrived at Marston around 1723, had a national reputation as a landscape gardener, and was an early advocate of replacing the formalities of French and Dutch gardens with a more natural style, although in a less thoroughgoing way than that later adopted by 'Capability' Brown.

It is likely that one of Switzer's first tasks was to design a building to stand on a small mound close to the Frome road. This was the **Temple of the Goddess Cloacina** which had a series of busts and statues in the Roman style, including one of Apollo. These disappeared in 1744 when the temple was converted into an ice-house; today it is used as a tool shed. An illustration in Vitruvius Britannicus shows the Temple in 1739 standing at the north-east corner of a formal garden consisting of a lawn and a parterre which was later replaced by naturalistic landscaping.

Two **Grottoes** were built around the same time. The first, dating from 1742, stood over a spring and was dedicated to Boyle's friend, Dr William King. It was drawn by the Reverend John Skinner in 1835 who described it as being 'near the spring nearly opposite the church at Marston'. This was the new church situated to the west of the house, and the drawing depicts the grotto with an irregular roof and a series of openings including a high central arch.

The other grotto stood at the northern edge of the parterre and was built over a spring in 1743. It survives today as an irregular, essentially oblong, structure made of coursed limestone rubble, and standing around three metres high. At the front is a large opening through which passed a path from the parterre. At the east end the walls are curved as if intended to surround a circular pool. However any trace of a pool has long since been erased and the structure has been largely reclaimed by nature, with trees growing out of the roof. Surrounding it is a low line of irregular stones covered with moss, which may once have formed part of the building.

A Grotto at Marston House, dating from 1743

The grotto was built by James Scott, who, according to Lady Orrery, was slow completing it. In a letter to her husband, she complained that 'Scott [has] left us [and] my grotto is a very little way advanced'. Boyle continued to add follies to the estate over the next 30 years. These included a labyrinth, several fountains and a group of statues, including one of Bacchus set in a wooden cabinet. There was also a seat, which, according to letter written by Boyle to Tom Southerne in 1733, had 'two little closets where you and Phillis may whisper your loves, and where I may count my beads and say my Mattins'. None of these features has survived.

One that does, albeit in a relatively poor state, is **Lady Cork's Bath** which probably dates from the 1740s. Once elegant, it affected the air of a Roman temple, classical in style and with a mock cemetery with sham gravestones complementing it. Made of local Doulting stone, it had a pediment and was entered through a Doric arch with keystone and impost mouldings. Little remains of this embellishment today and only its west wall retains its original height of about three metres at the point of its gable, under which is a curved arch and a window either side. The remaining walls enclose a plunge pool, over a metre deep, still actively fed by a spring, and a rubble arch, probably added later, stands to one side. When Bishop Pococke visited Marston in 1754, he described the bath as looking as though it were 'in the enclosure of an ancient cemetery, with several old inscriptions made for it … At the end is a small room very elegantly furnished; this I take to be Lady Orrery's place of retirement.' Today, with another small pond on its south side and a fernery established nearby, it lies within the curtilage of the old gardener's cottage (now known as Home Farm), built around 1775.

Marston's glory has been substantially restored after many years of neglect. Although some of the outlying buildings, including the boathouse on the lake, are still derelict and overgrown, the house was bought in 1984 by Foster Yeoman Ltd, the quarrying company, with the deliberate intention of conserving a piece of Somerset's heritage. They turned the house into their head office, employing Warminster builders R Butcher & Son, thanks to whom it now stands resplendent on its slight rise overlooking the Vale of Witham.

MIDFORD

There are several theories about how **Midford Castle** (ST759613) came to be built, although none is conclusive. It has been claimed that it was built as the result of a winning bet on the ace of clubs, that it was based on a design in the Builder's Magazine, even that it was somehow linked with wild orgies in the nearby Priory. These stories have given the place the reputation of being something of an oddity, which it is, but only in its ace-of-clubs groundplan, and not in the proclivities of its owners or visitors. As regards the first theory, it has been suggested that Henry Woolhouse Disney Roebuck wished to celebrate his luck with the ace of clubs at the gaming table by building a house in the same shape, but this story did not appear in print before 1899 when W Jones Hunt wrote an article for the Bath Weekly Argus. The truth may simply be that Roebuck was a wealthy romantic who chose the plan and design for aesthetic reasons.

The Gatehouse, Midford Castle

The stories aside, Midford Castle is an impressive building standing at the top of a rise overlooking the Midford Valley, a narrow combe down which the Midford Brook runs to the River Avon. The **Gatehouse** (ST756613), with its crenellations and turrets made of local stone, gives a foretaste of the main building. The drive leads down to the Castle which strikes the visitor

Midford Castle

with more elaborate features: trefoil plan, crenellations, windows with ogee drip-moulds, and quatrefoil openings in the parapet suggesting a solid storey, but with nothing behind. Midford Castle is no sham, however; it was always intended as a family home, and has been occupied almost continuously since it was built.

Roebuck was born Henry Woolhouse Disney in 1733, the son of a Notting-hamshire physician, and took the name of his uncle, John Roebuck, when he inherited his estates in Yorkshire. When he died in 1796, an obituary described him as 'fond of his pleasure boat [and] one of the first gentleman mariners of the age'. It may have been on his second marriage to Elizabeth Bayliss in 1774 that he decided to build Midford Castle; the style of its internal decoration supports a date of around 1775. The architect is unknown, although it may have been John Carter, who published a design for a 'Gothick Mansion to be Erected on an Eminence that Commands an Extensive Prospect' in The Builder's Magazine in 1774. Although Midford Castle displays elements of this design, it has an extra storey with ogee windows and a large terrace basement.

Carter, who had worked for James Wyatt, was an artist and antiquarian as well as an architect; he was also the editor of the Builder's Magazine. He was on good terms with Horace Walpole and had made numerous sketches of Strawberry Hill,

Walpole's Gothick mansion at Twickenham. Because of this connection, Carter has also been proposed as the architect of the Priory, the mock church near the Castle, whose twin towers – one slender and one broad – resemble the coupling of the towers at Strawberry Hill. As regards the trefoil plan of the Castle, Carter would almost certainly have known Blaise Castle near Bristol which had been built for Thomas Farr in 1766 as an eyecatcher.

The Castle sits on a terrace with a curving balustrade pierced with quatrefoil openings, which forms the roof of the basement. This was originally intended to house offices and the servants' quarters, but because of its almost complete lack of windows the rooms were dark and gloomy, and the servants were soon relocated to the Priory. Entering the Castle by the door from the carriage drive, a small lobby leads into the hall, which is shaped like a diamond because it was the space left in the middle after the towers on each side were built. These towers, each of which contains a large living room on the ground floor, form the shape of the 'club'. Approached by a spiral staircase, the most charming feature of the first-floor rooms are their decorative plasterwork ceilings, probably by Thomas Stocking of Bristol. Here we see motifs typical of his style, with bay leaves and roses intertwined, and small birds flying around the spaces in between.

Collinson described how, 'on the north and east sides of the house, is a very deep narrow sequestered glen, the steep narrow sides of which are clothed with fine coppice woods intersected with beautiful walks ornamented with flowering shrubs'. Here can be found the **Priory**, which, Collinson informs us, had

> Gothick windows and a circular embattled tower, in which is a commodious tea-room and offices below. At a little distance from this, under a thick mass of shade, stands a rustic hermitage on the brow of the steep descent. The whole surrounding scenery is highly picturesque and romantick.

Early photographs reveal that the Priory had two towers next to if not joined to each other, one short and thick, the other tall and thin with a conical roof. In 1944, when Christopher Hussey visited the Priory for Country Life, he described its 'nave' with a large fireplace, niches in the side walls for candles, high windows and a veranda around the base. Similarities to features in the Castle, such as ogee heads to the niches, further support the theory that John Carter designed the Priory as well as the Castle. Today the Priory is a sad ruin. A broken tower has fallen prey to graffiti artists; apart from that, little more than the vague outline of foundation stones can be seen. Of the hermitage there is no trace.

Such was the reverence for the Gothick style and spirit of place in both the Castle and the Priory that one must conclude that Roebuck was more interested in creating a romantic retreat than in any profligacy.

MONTACUTE

Montacute (ST499170), with its late Elizabethan mansion, is one of Somerset's most celebrated estates. Before the National Trust took the property over, it was owned by the Phelips family for 400 years. Their most illustrious member was Sir Edward Phelips, Speaker of the House of Commons from 1604 to 1611 and then Master of the Rolls until his death in 1614. He rebuilt the house, but it was after his death that the garden took the shape that we see today.

Jacobean splendour at Montacute

The forecourt of the house was based on the original medieval fortified house, and the two magnificent corner **Pavilions**, built around 1638, replaced castellated bastions. Although their two sets of windows indicate they were built with two floors, each now consists of a single room. Originally, the pavilions contained bedrooms on the upper floors, but were later converted to game larders, with the floors being removed to create sufficient height to hang game. They have bay windows with lozenge-leaded panes and are decorated with corner obelisks and a Flemish-style parapet. Their roofs are ogee-shaped and topped with a finial in the shape of two rings. This motif is echoed in the small, open gazebos situated half way along the balustrades. There were once other outbuildings including a pigeon house, gatehouses and a banqueting house 'arched with freestone, wainscoted within and leaded on the top thereof', but these have all gone.

Overlooking Montacute from the west is **St Michael's Tower** (ST493169). It stands on 'Mons Acutus', the site of a castle built by Robert, Count of Mortain, the half-brother of William the Conqueror, and later of a chapel attached

to the nearby priory. In 1760, Edward Phelips V decided to build a circular Ham-stone tower on the hill. It is about five metres in diameter and rises straight for about 15 metres before curving inwards for three metres to a viewing platform. Above the entrance is a Greek inscription which can be translated as 'a house built in 1760 – a look-out tower'. Inside is a 52-step spiral staircase, poorly lit by a couple of narrow window slits.

St Michaels' Tower on an early twentieth-century postcard and as it appears today

NEMPNETT THRUBWELL

The Ordnance Survey map and many other authoritative sources insist that the **Nempnett Needle** (ST549604) is an obelisk. However, while it has an authentically Egyptian look, it is in fact it is a ventilation shaft for a water pipeline built in 1846. Around 10 metres high, and tapering to a triangular top, it stands beside the road from Nempnett Thrubwell to Chew Stoke, and is built of limestone. Ventilation is provided by two rectangular openings near the top. A plate on the base of the obelisk bears the enigmatic message 'LOW 42' which

The Nempnett Needle

presumably has some significance in water-speak. A metal plate nearby covers what may be another shaft. These small features add to the mystery of the Nempnett Needle and make it one of those relics of a bygone industrial age which modern man does not fully understand, thereby helping it to gain the 'folly' label.

NETHER STOWEY

Stowey Court (ST195397) was begun by Lord James Audley in 1495, and completed by his great-grandson in 1588. The walls around the gardens contain fragments from a fourteenth-century building as well as a striking **Gazebo**. Its date and builder are unknown but it features in an estate plan of 1750 and may have been added in the 1730s or 40s when the estate was owned by Robert Everard.

A well-known landmark on the side of a busy road, its lower half is made of stone and its upper half of brick. The door from the garden is faintly Venetian in style. Each wall has a pair of sash windows and it is topped by a particularly fine ogee roof with a ball finial complemented by a chimney. Although still in good condition, it suffers from damp, mainly on its sun-starved northern side where two openings lead to an undercroft.

The Gazebo at Nether Stowey before the First World War.
The road is somewhat busier today

NEWTON ST LOE

The Langton family's association with **Newton Park** (ST695641) lasted some two and a half centuries, starting in 1666 when Bristol Merchant Venturer Joseph Langton bought the estate of Newton Court, as it was then known. It was a place with an ancient pedigree, including a medieval castle keep which is still in use today. The main house, however, was built in the 1760s.

The Temple at Newton Park

The landscape below the house on the west side is of particular interest, as it remains almost exactly as laid out by 'Capability' Brown. Later, Humphry Repton also worked at Newton Park, creating two large lakes surrounded by dense woodland and sloping lawns. After these distinguished interventions, the landscape was allowed to deteriorate for nearly 200 years until the 1990s when a grant of £300,000 was made by the Heritage Lottery Fund, and Nicholas Pearson Associates were commissioned to put together a landscape structure plan. The project included the rebuilding of the **Garden Temple**, also known as the Orangery, a relatively plain five-arched building with a pediment. Its age is uncertain, although it almost certainly dates from before 1789, when the last vestiges of a formal garden layout – a grand double avenue – were swept away. Its setting as the focal point of complex interlinking views between the house, the old castle keep and various paths, as well as its location by the upper lake, suggest that Brown had a hand its design.

The Temple appears in nineteenth-century photographs, when it had sash windows which could be taken out on hot summer days. However, by 1959 it was in a very poor state, having been struck by a falling elm which effectively demolished one side. When the site was cleared all that was left of the building was the base of the back and side walls. Architect Charles Johnstone of the Heritage Practice rebuilt the Garden Temple to the original design, although without the sash windows. Its arches will probably remain open, with stone seats placed inside. There are also plans to restore a nearby Boathouse which is still largely intact.

OAKHILL

Little stirs nowadays in Harridge Wood which lies in a deep, damp valley and forms a small nature reserve, a haven of seclusion for wildlife east of Oakhill. In the eighteenth century, however, it was a hive of industry. It formed part of the estate of John Billingsley, the agricultural reformer who built Ashwick Grove House

nearby. When he dammed the stream to provide power for a series of mills, he had one eye on the picturesque nature of the setting. Now that the mills have gone, the mill leats, waterfalls and bridges he constructed remain to delight walkers through this secluded valley.

Billingsley also built a three-arched **Grotto** (ST646477), carved out of the rock and commanding a prospect of one of the most attractive stretches of his demesne. Looking south across the wooded valley, it stands some eight feet high and twenty feet long. It is now covered in moss and ferns, with boulders, which may once have formed part of the roof, scattered on the ground. Half a mile down the valley to the east is a ruinous mill in the form of a **Gothic Cottage** (ST652479), which now harbours a colony of bats. With the demolition of Ashwick Grove House in the mid-twentieth century, this pair of abandoned and atmospheric follies are all that remain to remind us of one of Somerset's most famous eighteenth-century figures.

Lost follies of Mendip: John Billingsley's Grotto and Gothic Cottage

The **Pondsmead** estate at Oakhill (ST634467) was developed in the nineteenth century by the Jillards and later by the Spencers, both of whom owed their prosperity to the success of the Oakhill Brewery, one of the largest in the west of England. It was claimed that the water from a local spring was particularly suitable for brewing a stout with medicinal properties which rejoiced in the name of Oakhill Invalid Stout. Evidence of the source of this life-enhancing drink can be seen on a 1822 map which shows the stream running through the estate of Mr Jillard, who acquired the brewery around 1810.

The lakes on the estate, however, were not created until after the house was rebuilt in 1874. Several curious buildings were erected at around the same time, not all of which have survived. The main part of the **Rustic Summerhouse**, for example – a cottage orné with a conical thatched roof supported by rubble walls – has gone. The three depressed arch-head windows had stained glass at the top of each light, while three further windows had ogee heads. The door on the east side had rustic panels and was covered by a thatched 'bonnet' supported on rustic posts. The interior, according to the Listed Buildings Record, contained 'fine carved wood fireplace surrounds, matching those in the house'. Although the Summerhouse has gone, a small outbuilding which used to be attached to it and was built in a similar style, has survived. This plain, unadorned building is open on three sides and has a thatched roof supported on rustic columns. It is currently used to store garden machinery.

The best-known building at Pondsmead is a circular **Lodge**, still in use as

The Lodge at Pondsmead

a dwelling house. It is striking for its rough-hewn construction, with monumental rockwork jutting out raggedly on all sides, and eaves which sweep up at odd angles. Consisting mainly of tufa, with a hipped slate roof, it has a single storey and attic with dormer windows. Its air of rusticity is enhanced by the branch-like surrounds to the door and the tracery of the windows of the entrance porch, which also boasts some simple shell-work.

The **Grotto** is even more rugged-looking. Forming part of the dam between the upper and lower lakes, it consists of a long screen built of rough-hewn random limestone, around 50 metres wide and three metres high. Inside is a bewilderingly irregular series of tunnels, staircases and niches, with a ruined arch and viewing platform, and water running through at various points. Some of the water drips away through the rock, although most of it is channelled between high stone walls at the east end of the grotto, before tumbling down a four-metre-high waterfall. One of the tunnels meanders for about 25 metres past gaping holes, invading vegetation and through Stygian damp and gloom until light is seen at the eastern end.

Another intriguing feature is a vaulted **Hermit's Cell** which is approached from the landing stage on the lower lake. It seems more suitable for a social gathering than as a hermitage: there are eight niches for sitting and two more stone seats at a squarish table, while stalactite-like rocks jut down from the ceiling. To the west is another chamber about two metres high and three metres long, with seven niches carved out of the rock. The romance continues with a winding staircase, again with niches and seats, leading to an upper level. A little window looks out over the lower lake, and eventually the staircase opens out onto the upper lake. The view from the top over the lower lake is slightly obscured by the trees that are now higher than the grotto, but it is clear that this is a structure of Herculean proportions which would have afforded an intriguing focus of pleasure during its heyday.

ORCHARDLEIGH

Lullington and Orchardleigh
What a peace steals over me
Born of happy memory...
Lullington and Orchardleigh
England as it used to be
CBL Haslewood, 1937

Bankruptcy, general degradation and the conversion of much of the estate to a golf course have taken their toll on Orchardleigh, so it is all the more remarkable that its follies have survived. For long in the hands of the Champneys family, by the early nineteenth century, when Sir Thomas Champneys was the owner, the estate was irredeemably encumbered with debt. In 1814 he was forced to convey the reversionary interest to one Richard Henry Cox, while remaining tenant for life. Lord Hylton of Ammerdown (qv) called Champneys 'a lesser Beckford', probably because he did not have the Caliph of Fonthill's means, nor his stylistic panache. Champneys, like Beckford, however, liked to build imprudently on the grand scale.

The trouble was that Champneys carried on spending. In 1816, he built **Gloucester Lodge** (ST786518), ostensibly for the visit of the Duke of Gloucester, but also to outshine John Houlton's newly-completed Bath Lodge at nearby Farleigh House (qv). Also known as the Lullington Gatehouse, sale particulars drawn up in 1849 described it as 'a noble Gothic erection, having a beautiful groined arch thrown over the road, with strong massive gates'.

Regency extravagance in deepest Somerset:
Gloucester Lodge and the Temple Boathouse at Orchardleigh

The gatehouse has two pairs of machicolated octagonal stair turrets rising on either side of a broad depressed carriage arch, with latticework wooden gates in the style of a portcullis. Set over the arch is another piece of Champneys fantasy designed to give his family an air of antiquity which it did not merit – a stone inscribed '1485', the date of the Battle of Bosworth Field. On the inner side of the gatehouse is a coat of arms flanked by four heraldic shields to remind the visitor of the pedigree of the owner, but which were probably spurious. To the left is a three-storey square tower with a projecting round turret in one corner; to the right is a simpler round tower with crenellations. The flanking walls curve for some considerable way towards the public road creating a courtyard with lawns on either side of the carriage drive. On the perimeter by the road are two more square turrets, or massive gate piers, over three metres high and with projecting battlements. They have blind arches above which is a blank panel for a coat of arms, and give the impression that they are gatehouses, although they are pure sham, having no gates themselves, merely acting as a prelude to the bigger sham a hundred metres away.

In 1854, the estate was bought by William Duckworth, a Lancastrian entrepreneur. The old house was demolished and replaced by a one designed by TH Wyatt, while the park was relandscaped by William Page and later by William Thomas. The gatehouse survived, however, as did the estate's crowning glory, a serpentine lake covering 24 acres and supplied, according to the 1849 sale particulars, by 'never failing springs, abounding with fish'. On the margin of the lake stands a **Temple** (ST782510), which appears on plans drawn up in 1818-19, and described in the sale particulars as 'a retreat for the enjoyment of fishing and commanding rich and enchanting views of the adjoining lovely scenery'. In the Ionic style, it has a smooth ashlar front and a slate roof, under which runs a frieze and moulded cornice. It is in a sad state: part of the pediment is supported by a wooden frame; elsewhere the fabric is cracking and being invaded by vegetation.

The terrace in front of the Temple forms the roof of a **Boathouse**. The front corners of this roof have stepped plinths, which may at one time have supported statues. The Boathouse is mainly built of irregular quarry-faced ashlar stone blocks, with a round arch through which boats headed out onto the lake. The lake, like the boathouse, has seen better days, having receded to such an extent that the bed inside the boathouse is dry, its entrance screened by reeds and choked by water-lilies.

PORLOCK

At **Ashley Combe** (SS856482), high above Porlock, is one of Somerset's most intriguing lost gardens. Evidence of it can be seen by walkers en route from Porlock to Culbone in the shape of two overgrown tunnels, separated by a couple of hundred metres, one of which has a small turret attached to it. These are the last easily visible vestiges of a great estate that once covered this hillside.

The history of Ashley Combe stretches back several centuries, but things only started to stir when William King, 8th Baron King and later the 1st Earl of Lovelace, inherited the estate in the early nineteenth century. In 1835 he married the Honourable Augusta Ada Byron, the daughter of the poet. Her talents were

The Gatehouse at Ashley Combe is in a good state of repair,
but the Terraces and the Belvedere marking the far corner of the garden are slowly being
reclaimed by nature

not poetical but mathematical and scientific, and she devised some of the first computer programmes for an analytical machine using punch cards developed by Charles Babbage.

It was in honour of Babbage that the Philosopher's Walk was constructed as part of King's wildly ambitious plans for developing the estate. King was an architect and engineer, and not only received the approval of the Institute of Civil Engineers for his pioneering work developing steam-bent arched trusses but also won a medal for brickmaking at the Great Exhibition in 1851. Soon after his marriage to Ada, he determined to make Ashley Combe a showpiece of architectural design. Inspired by what he had seen around the Italian Lakes, he built a house with a clock tower in the form of a Renaissance campanile and a garden with multi-arched terraces, vaults and, most significantly, tunnels. King was obsessed with making Ashley Combe as private as possible – one of his aims was to make the estate 'a hermitage worthy of [Ada's] presence' – and tunnels were a crucial part of his design. He built a similar network of tunnels at Horsley Towers, his estate in Surrey. Tradesmen calling at Ashley House would enter the estate via the charming gatehouse, which still survives, before wending their way up the hillside through a series of tunnels to emerge at the back of the house. In this way an air of mystery was preserved, a kind of separateness that kept local people in awe.

When King sent his wife the plans for Ashley Combe, she replied, 'your drawings of Ashley Combe excite my curiosity about the bastions and battlements. You must have fancied yourself a feudal lord.' Its glory was to be short-lived, however. After King was made Lord Lieutenant for Surrey in 1840, he spent less and less time in Somerset. Ashley Combe slipped into a gradual decline and the spell was finally broken when Ada died in 1852 at the early age of 37. King's heirs treated the place very much as a holiday home, spending little on its upkeep. Eventually it was let, first as a Barnardo's home, and later as a country club run along the lines of a YMCA. After that closed, the building swiftly deteriorated and was finally demolished around 1960.

Since then, vegetation has gradually gripped the estate in its stranglehold, with trees growing up to obscure the view, tunnels falling in and many garden features being obliterated by invasive plants.

However, there still remain three remarkable long terraces in an L-shape. Most of the arches in the terraces are blind, although some lead to vaults which may have been used for storage. Above them is a large circular, squat tower, medieval in style, whose staircase one can use to ascend or descend the terraces. At the opposite end of what was once the garden is a small turret with a conical roof. It stands like a belvedere marking the far corner of the garden's lower level, although the view of the coast is now obscured by trees. The atmosphere is very much of a lost world, overrun by ever-encroaching vegetation, on the foothills of Exmoor.

REDLYNCH

The **Chequers Towers** (ST685324) are a comparatively straightforward gate-way guarding the north-west corner of the estate of Redlynch House, originally built in the seventeenth century but demolished in 1913-14 after a fire and rebuilt in 1932. The gateway, which probably dates from the mid-eighteenth cen-

tury, consists of two circular battlemented towers joined by a pointed arch, with Y-tracery in their lower windows and quatrefoil windows above. Here, the style of the Middle Ages is enhanced by the Ilchester arms which flank the central arch on both sides. The crest has three foxes' heads on a chevron set in a field of fleurs-de-lys, surmounted by a chapeau, or a cap of dignity, and a further large fleur-de-lys on the dexter chief.

The gateway may have been commissioned by Sir Stephen Fox, who was elevated to the peerage and became the 1st Lord Ilchester in the 1750s, to impress George III who often stayed at Redlynch on his way to Weymouth to take the waters. The architect is unknown, but Henry Flitcroft, who carried out work at Redlynch in the 1750s, and who built Alfred's Tower at Brewham (qv), is a possible candidate.

Today the fabric is starting to crack up, a buttress has been erected to prevent the collapse of the western tower, and ivy is encroaching. A further ignominy – which nevertheless enhances the building's status as a folly – is the diversion of the driveway around the arch, so that it no longer serves as a gateway.

STRATTON-ON-THE FOSSE

The idea of the ferme ornée never really took hold in Somerset, but at Manor Farm, a little to the north of Stratton-on-the Fosse, there are a couple of embellishments which add a certain character to the place. Situated in the front courtyard is the most prominent of these, the **Bell Tower** (ST666517), built by William Beauchamp, a local brewer. This nine-metre-high structure tapers in four stages towards a belfry containing a bell from the brewery. The next level down used to have a clock, but this has gone; below this are carved the initials and date 'WB 1903'. A solid square base supports the tower, which has had to be buttressed to stabilise the structure.

There is also a **Sham Façade** which originally stood at the front of

the farmhouse but has since been moved around the side. Although it looks like the front of a classical garden shed, on opening the door it is found to lead directly into the rear garden. It consists of four Doric columns surmounted by a pediment with a fleur-de-lys in the tympanum and inscribed with the motto 'Ich Dien', the date 1883 and the initials 'AE', commemorating a visit by Albert Edward, Prince of Wales.

STREET

Before architectural reclamation became big business, landowners with gardens to fill had to hunt around for follies on decayed estates. One such endangered building, a Doric portico, once stood at the head of a flight of steps leading to the

Clark's Folly

front door of Westcombe House between Frome and Bruton. When the house was scheduled for demolition in 1956, it seemed likely that the portico would follow it into oblivion. Before the contractors moved in, however, Stephen Clark went to take one last look at it with his father, the owner of C & J Clark's, the Street-based shoe manufacturers. He later recalled that, 'as we regarded the front of the house, deplored the destruction and admired the portico, my father said, "If I were 40 years younger, I should do something about that." As I was about 40 years younger, I decided to try to do something.'

The cost of dismantling what became known as **Clark's Folly** (ST491372), moving it to Street, storing and re-erecting it, constructing a brick backdrop and paying the architect's fees amounted to some £833. Modifications to the building included the installation of an asbestos ceiling and lead guttering. Situated at the end of a double row of Lombardy poplars and walnut trees 'in the landscape of Bowlingreen Factory', it is reminiscent of a classical temple or eyecatcher meant to be seen from some great house. Although it no longer serves its original function as a gateway, a black-painted metal rack at the back indicates that it still serves one practical use – feeding hay to cattle.

UPTON

Lady Harriet's Drive was built in the late eighteenth century so that the widowed Lady Acland could travel easily from her home at Wiveliscombe to visit her daughter, the Countess of Carnarvon, at Pixton. **Haddon Lodge** (SS988287), otherwise known as the Pepperpot Castle, was built on the drive in the early nineteenth century. It is roughly triangular, with hexagonal towers at the corners, blind lancets, quatrefoil and Gothic windows and a crenellated parapet. It was enlarged in the twentieth century and is covered in white render. Altogether, it is a charming building and a delightful exercise in restrained Gothicism.

WALTON-IN-GORDANO

Although there is some dispute over the date of **Walton Castle** (ST415728), it is now generally accepted that, despite its medieval style, it was built around 1620, probably as a hunting lodge. In Parks and Gardens of Somerset, James Bond states that it was built by the 1st Lord Poulett after inheriting the estate through his marriage to Elizabeth Ken in 1614. Although he also enclosed some of the land on the estate, he did not settle at Walton for any length of time as his main estates were at Hinton St George and Buckland. It seems likely, given its subsequent history, that Walton Castle was still unfinished when England descended into the turmoil of the Civil War in the 1640s. Lord Poulett, along with his son, were supporters of the King. After being captured at the Siege of Exeter, they had to pay a large sum of money to escape prosecution. Financial constraints, along with the straitened climate of the Cromwellian interregnum, would hardly have been conducive to lavishing enormous sums on buildings intended purely for pleasure.

Above, Walton Castle around 1900, abandoned to the elements; below, the eptimome of the picturesque ruin: a Victorian lady reclines against a tree to contemplate the castle

Walton Castle was abandoned and by 1813, when Joseph Nightingale visited, he reported that 'the roof and floor are now fallen in, and a great part of the walls are going fast to decay'. Not until the 1990s did a new owner finally reverse centuries of decay, elaborating its baronial air in the process. At the outer entrance, the visitor is greeted by a pair of black dragons with red tongues and crosses on their wings. Through the outer door one enters a courtyard where there is another pair of dragons and an old bench on which it is claimed that the Magna Carta was signed. An octagonal keep, with an octagonal turret attached to it, is surrounded by an octagonal curtain wall with round crenellated turrets at each corner. The turrets, originally intended just for ornament, now serve a variety of functions, housing a television projection room, a utility room and a games room. Although the keep has also been modernised with modern conveniences such as a kitchen, bathrooms and so on, the plasterwork on the ceilings has a satisfyingly ancient look to it.

WELLINGTON

When Arthur Wellesley was elevated to the peerage in 1809, he took the title Viscount of Wellington and Talavera. Talavera was the site of a famous victory in the Peninsula War, Wellington the town in Somerset near one of his estates. After his victory at Waterloo there was a wave of enthusiasm to commemorate him, and in 1817, at the instigation of William Ayshford Sanford of Nynehead, Thomas Lee produced the design for a **Wellington Monument** (ST137172) on the Duke's land high on the Blackdown Hills. When the foundation stone for what was intended as a massive column was laid in October 1817, bands, standard bearers, artillery carriages, 60 horsemen and 10,000 onlookers were present. In his address, the chairman of the monument committee, Lord Somerville, referred to two Somerset follies, the Burton Pynsent Monument and Alfred's Tower:

> The spot chosen for this purpose is well suited to keep alive the remembrance of splendid victories gained by this hero, and cannot fail, at the same time, to perpetuate the invincible courage of those who fought under his command. It will, moreover, form a most prominent feature in a part of England already ornamented by the pillar raised in honour of the late Earl of Chatham and the tower built at Stourhead in commemoration of the spot where Alfred the Great first erected his standard.

There were plans for a cast-iron statue of the Duke in a commanding pose at the top of the monument and three cottages, to be occupied by three army veterans – an Englishman, an Irishman and a Scotsman – at the bottom. Despite the initial enthusiasm, however, the scheme soon ran into financial difficulties as the Duke's popularity in the area started to wane. He certainly did not attempt to court it, visiting the town from which he had taken his title only once, in 1819. During the Reform Riots a few years later, his opposition to the Reform Bill saw a further downturn in his popularity. At one stage, a local pub named after him had its sign removed and returned with a picture of the devil alongside that of the Duke. The project ground to a halt in 1829, and the stump of stone, quarried at Whitestaunton near Chard, stood as a gaunt reminder of the fickleness of fortune until 1841 when it shattered after being struck by lightning.

After Wellington's death in 1852, the project was revived, this time using the plans of Henry Edmund Goodridge, the architect of Beckford's Tower in Bath (qv). It was completed the following year and in 1890 was restored and heightened by 1.5 metres, taking it to 53 metres. In the form of a triangular obelisk rather than a column, its pyramidal top is pierced by small windows which can be reached by a spiral staircase. There is a winged Egyptian-style panel above the entrance and the base is topped by prominent cornices. It was originally intended to surround the monument with cannons captured at Waterloo, but these never materialised. Four cannons were later installed around the base but these were taken away and melted down in the Second World War. The cannon that stands below the monument today was donated by Wellington Rotary Club in 1985.

WEST HORRINGTON

A corner of Somerset that is forever Rome

Not surprisingly, the Second World War was not a fruitful time for folly building in Somerset. However, one of the county's most intriguing follies came about as a direct consequence of the war. Despite being just four metres high, because of its location, on the side of the busy A39 near Pen Hill north of Wells, it has probably puzzled more people than most of the other follies featured in this book. It consists of a plinth supported by four columns decorated with crescents, on which **Romulus and Remus** (ST570490), the legendary founders of Rome, are being suckled by a she-wolf.

It was the work of Gaetano Celestra, an Italian prisoner of war who was interned at the nearby Penleigh Camp. When he was detailed, along with

123

other prisoners of war, to repair a wall damaged by bombing on the estate of Mr Wellstead-White, he managed to convince him that the wall should be embellished with the symbol of Rome. Built with plaster and concrete over a wire frame, it was apparently based on an image from an Italian banknote. Despite its somewhat unpropitious genesis it is an impressive piece of work which has stood the test of time remarkably well.

Celestra also left behind a flower basket and a pond as a thank you to the people of Somerset who had made him so welcome, despite the circumstances of his stay in the county. After the war he opted to stay on in Somerset, despite the entreaties of his wife in North Africa, working first on a farm and later for an Italian builder in Wells.

WESTON-SUPER-MARE

Shrubbery Avenue, just north of Weston town centre, is, as its name suggests, a pleasant but very ordinary suburban street. At one time, however, it was home to some rather colourful characters, such as the redoubtable Sophia Rooke. Bishop Law (qv Banwell) said of her, 'in this world there are two calamities – the Pope and Lady Rooke, and the latter is the greater evil'. Around 1847, she built the Villa Rosa along with some tunnels, a menagerie and bear pit, and an octagonal three-storey **Water Tower** (ST317623) which supplied water to nearby houses. Although the tunnels and the menagerie have disappeared, the medieval-style Tower survives. Built of sandstone rubble with freestone dressings, it is set on a ribbed course of stone, with blind cruciform arrowslits, elongated lancet windows and a crenellated parapet. High on the façade, sculptures of animals including lions and cows punctuate the corners of the octagon. A somewhat unsympathetic modern extension was added when it was converted to residential use, although its design does reflect the octagonal shape of the Tower.

Slyply is the name of a business set up by Bristol-based artist Graham Caine, offering 'utility sculptors', 'strokeable woodwork' and 'applyed [sic] artists'. Caine is the first to admit that 'plywood is an obsession for me … It's what I'm all about', and in his hands it is transformed from something unremarkable into forms that look as though they could have grown straight out of the ground. He has a long list of satisfied customers who know that they have something truly original, ranging from domestic items such as ashtrays or bookcases to staircases and even complete buildings.

One of Caine's most charming commissions is Margaret Burrow's **Summerhouse** (ST323624) at Hope Cottage in Weston-Super-Mare. In 1993, she was on a train from Bristol to Gloucester when she saw his plywood home in Boiling Wells Lane from the embankment at St Werburgh's. She sent her son along to find out more about it and before long Caine had a contract to build a summerhouse in her garden. A hobbit house, a Gaudiesque pixie house, a den are some of the terms than have been used to describe this building which stands beside the lawn in a secluded garden on a hill above Weston. About three metres high and two and a half metres wide, it is a hexagon with a pointed top like the hat of one of Snow White's dwarves. Six ribs made of Canadian spruce give it its basic shape and, reinforced by steel rods, they are sunk into concrete. The ribs meet at a central boss in the roof, and around the ribs, the walls have been constructed of concrete built up around a wire mesh to give it form and strength, and sculpted into curves. The door and window frames are of plywood, built up in layers and with a marked absence of straight lines. On three sides are windows with a variety of knobs and little trays jutting out. There's a knob, for example, to hang clothes on, and a small tray next

A poem in plywood:
Margaret Burrow's Summerhouse

to the bench for placing a watch, jewellery or glasses on before one reclines on a hot summer's afternoon, or indeed for the whole night, as Mrs Burrows does on occasion.

WEST QUANTOXHEAD

The house at St Audrie's in West Quantoxhead is superbly placed in a wide ravine between cliffs and surrounded by wide lawns which slope down towards the sea. Built in the eighteenth century by the Acland Family, and added to in the nineteenth, it was described when put up for sale in 1835 as 'suited to a man of rank'. Tucked away behind the house at the end of a terrace stands the **Shell Grotto** (ST111425), exuding an air of genteel decay, having been more or less abandoned for over a century. The 1835 sales particulars described this as 'a grotto of incomparable beauty full of fossils ingeniously placed … a subterranean cave with an infinity of pleasing objects, one and all proclaiming in language not to be misapprehended, that judgment and good taste must have presided at every council of deliberation'. This was, of course, written before the passing of the Property Misdescriptions Act, when estate agents waxed even more lyrical than they do today.

The subterranean nature of the Shell Grotto was actually a figment of the agent's imagination, possibly as a result of the gloom of the interior. The grotto was an oval building, entirely above ground at the end of the terrace wall, and the entrance was up a flight of four steps. It was built by two sisters, the Misses

Balch, and enough of their handiwork remains to give us a sense of how dazzling this little building must once have been. Entry is over a patterned pebble floor

and through a pointed arched doorway with octagonal diamond tracery. Although some of the stained glass in the door has gone, that in the window on the opposite side is largely intact. As for the ceiling, the pendant that once hung from it has long gone, and only stubs of the ornamental stalactites that decorated it remain. The walls, however, are still decorated with a rich variety of minerals and shells, included pieces of Watchet alabaster, exotic conches and a heart-shaped shell. The floor has a concentric pattern made mainly of pebbles with ammonites around the edge, designed to be admired no doubt by visitors sitting in niches around the walls.

An air of genteel decay:
St Audrie's Shell Grotto

It is said that the Bristol Channel could be seen from the window, but trees now obscure the view. A short distance away is a rock cave built around the same time. Set into the hillside, a rough stone arch forms the entrance, beyond which a short tunnel leads into a small room with a corbelled stone roof. Other features on the estate included a sea grotto on the shore, a fishing temple, a hermitage and an alcove. Although these have disappeared, there remain the cascades and waterfalls running through what the 1835 sale particulars described as 'thickly wooded groves and hollow glens … There is, throughout, such an air of tempered wildness as would gratify the eye of the lover of scenery, without offence to those who are inclined to look rather for evidences of the superintending hand of care and cultivation, and it may be added that if in this world we are allowed to approach elysium, it will not be far distant from St.Audrie's.'

WORLE

The **Observatory** (ST349633) at Worle has a chequered past. It was built around 1765 as a windmill, one of several that once stood on Worlebury Hill overlooking the sea. From around 1840 it was owned by William Rogers who also ran a bakery in Worle. In 1870, the bakery and the mill were advertised for sale in the Weston Mercury, but it was not until 1889 that the mill changed hands. The new owner stripped the mill of its sails, added an ogive roof, possibly to accommodate a telescope, placed a large cartouche over the entrance and built a house next door. A postcard from 1909 shows the roof ending in a ball finial and two ribbed bands of stone – one two-thirds of the way up and the other just below the crenellated parapet – encircling the tower.

Today the former windmill has changed yet again, almost beyond recognition. The house has gone and a modern one built ten metres or so away. The ogive roof has also gone, to be replaced by a flagpole, and the render on the walls has been restored and painted a brilliant white. The revamped tower did not, however, find favour with the anonymous author of a book published in the 1970s:

The Observatory in 1909; and as it appears today

> One could classify it loosely as a folly – but it is a rather muted example. For a folly proper should be built to outrage and shock: to ostentatiously revel in its own absurdity: to usurp the iron rule of function by expressing nothing bar its own quirky personality. Such buildings are the upshot of nervous energy and wealth. Considerable money is needed to render fancy corporate and three-dimensional, and the Worle Observatory pales beside the flagrant extravagances of Beckford and Horace Walpole. But it makes a satisfying decoration, like a chalk ornament atop a cake, a crenellated crown perching on the limestone ridge.

Muted or not, the Worle Observatory is a very pleasing ornament to the landscape, a landmark for miles around, and, unlike many follies, in an extremely good state of repair. The judgement of this anonymous critic seems unreasonably harsh. After all, if the creations of Beckford and Walpole were to be used as a benchmark to judge other follies by, how many would come up to scratch? Follies are follies not by virtue of their size or how much they cost, but because somebody had an overwhelming desire to build something with questionable functionality. While Stan Larcombe's *jeu d'esprit*, with which we started our peregrination, may not rank alongside Beckford's Tower, Sham Castle or Jack the Treacle Eater in terms of size, it would be folly to deny it a place alongside them in the rich gallimaufry that makes up Somerset Follies.

BIBLIOGRAPHY

Barton, Stuart, *Monumental Follies*, Worthing, Lyle Publications, 1972

Bush, Robin, *Somerset: The Complete Guide*, Wimborne, Dovecote Press, 1994

Collinson, John, *History and Antiquities of Somersetshire*, 3 vols, Bath, R Cruttwell, 1791

Cooke, Robert, *West Country Houses*, Dorchester, R Cooke, 1957

Darke, Jo, *The Monument Guide to England & Wales*, London, Macdonald, 1991

Dunning, Robert, *Some Somerset Country Houses*, Wimborne, Dovecote Press, 1991

Jones, Barbara, *Follies and Grottoes*, London, Constable, 1974

Hansell, Peter & Jean, *Doves and Dovecotes*, Bath, Millstream Books, 1987

Headley, Gwyn & Wim Meulenkamp, *Follies* (2nd Edition), London, Aurum Press, 1999

Jackson, Neil, *Nineteenth Century Bath: Architects and Architecture*, Bath, Ashgrove Press, 1991

Lansdown, Henry Venn, *Recollections of the Late William Beckford of Fonthill, Wilts and Lansdown, Bath*, Bath, privately printed, 1893

Lees-Milne, James, *William Beckford*, Tisbury, Compton Russell, 1976

Mowl, Tim, *Palladian Bridges*, Bath, Millstream Books, 1993

Mowl, Tim & Brian Earnshaw, *John Wood, Architect of Obsession*, Bath, Millstream Books, 1988

Mowl, Tim & Brian Earnshaw, *Trumpet at a Distant Gate*, London, Waterstone, 1985

Nightingale, Rev Joseph, *The Beauties of England & Wales*, Vol XIII, London, J Harris, 1813

Pevsner, Nikolaus, *The Buildings of England: North Somerset & Bristol*, Harmondsworth, Penguin, 1958

Pevsner, Nikolaus, *The Buildings of England: South & West Somerset*, Harmondsworth, Penguin, 1958

Roche, Rev. Brother J S, *A History of Prior Park College*, London, Burns, Oates & Washbourne, 1931

Snaddon, Brenda, *The Last Promenade: Sydney Gardens, Bath*, Bath, Millstream Books, 2000

Whitelaw, Jeffery W, *Follies* (2nd Edition), Princes Risborough, Shire Publications, 1997

Wood, John, *Essay Towards a Description of Bath* (2nd Edition), London, Bathoe & Lowndes, 1765

Young, Arthur, *Six Weeks Tour through the Southern Counties of England & Wales*, London, W Nicholl, 1768

The following publications have also been used: Royal Commission for Historic Monuments; Victoria County History; Country Life; Follies magazine (Journal of the Folly Fellowship); Garden History (Journal of the Garden History Society

About the Folly Fellowship

The Folly Fellowship was founded in 1988 as a pressure group to protect, preserve, and promote follies, grottoes & garden buildings. Initially a group of enthusiasts keen to record what was at first seen as a peculiarly British aspect of architecture, it has grown into a serious conservation and consultative architectural heritage charity, while not losing sight of the basic idea that these buildings are fun - they were built for pleasure before purpose. Some make us laugh, some provoke contemplative thoughts, some can frighten. Some are mere whims, others demand to be taken seriously.

People take their pleasures seriously - why should buildings be any different? An early realisation was the international flavour of the genre although the British Isles can count more follies per square mile than any other region, there are examples to be found all over the world.

In recent years, there has been an increased awareness of the importance of these buildings to our landscapes. Many have been restored and several have been completely rebuilt with local support. Better still, some individuals with imagination and the tenacity to fight the planning process, have begun to build new follies.

For more information about the Folly Fellowship visit the website (www.follies.org.uk) or contact: The Membership Secretary, Folly Fellowship, 36 Longfield Drive, Rodley, Leeds LS13 1JX

OTHER BOOKS FROM AKEMAN PRESS

THE MYTHMAKER:
John Wood 1704-1754
by Kirsten Elliott   £10

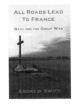

ALL ROADS LEAD TO FRANCE:
Bath & the Great War
by Andrew Swift   £30 (hardback)

THE RINGING GROOVES OF CHANGE:
Brunel & the Coming of the Railway to Bath
by Andrew Swift   £12

BATH PUBS
by Kirsten Elliott & Andrew Swift   £12.99

THE LOST PUBS OF BATH
by Kirsten Elliott & Andrew Swift   £15

AWASH WITH ALE:
2000 Years of Imbibing in Bath
by Kirsten Elliott & Andrew Swift   £12.99

Available from bookshops or post free from:
Akeman Press, 58 Minster Way, Bath BA2 6RL
www.akemanpress.com